TIMES FLIES . . .
AND TAKES THE BODY WITH IT.

The first time I went to the Mayo Clinic, at the age of forty-four, the doctor in charge of my physical said, "You have the body of a man of thirty-eight."

"Really?" I said. "Someone that old?"

"Yes, your heart is beating like Buddy Rich."

On my second visit, however, when I was forty-nine, the doctor in charge of my physical said, "You have the body of a man of forty-nine."

At least he hadn't said a *woman* of forty-nine. Nonetheless, I had aged eleven years in five, a thought that left me in despair; but then he said, "Mr. Cosby, were you an athlete?"

"Oh *yes*," I said with a happy leap of my morale. So my varsity muscles were still there.

"That's what I thought," the doctor said, "when I saw all the scars."

"So, doctor, give it to me straight: what do you think?"

"Oh, everything is normal."

"Well, *that's* good."

"Yes, if you died tomorrow, no one would be surprised."

BILL COSBY
TIME FLIES

Introduction by
Alvin F. Poussaint, M.D.

BANTAM BOOKS
NEW YORK • TORONTO • LONDON • SYDNEY • AUCKLAND

TIME FLIES
A Bantam Book / published by arrangement with Doubleday

PUBLISHING HISTORY
Doubleday edition published September 1987
Bantam edition / December 1988

ISBN 0-553-27724-3

Published simultaneously in the United States and Canada

PRINTED IN THE UNITED STATES OF AMERICA

20 19 18 17 16 15

*To my wife and my children,
and my mother and father
who can see the change.*

Contents

Contents

Francis Bacon said, "Age appears to be best in four things: old wood best to burn, old wine to drink, old friends to trust, and old authors to read."

This is only my second book, but I am definitely an older author. Younger than Francis Bacon, but older than I was when I wrote *Fatherhood*.

Am I now an authority on age? Well, I know nothing about gerontology except how to spell it. What I have put in this book is simply a report on the current state of a man who arrived in 1937, just ten days before the birth of Superman. But for me, the only thing that flies is time.

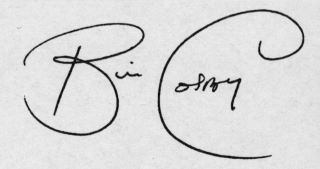

TIME FLIES

Introduction

by Alvin F. Poussaint, M.D.

*I am not afraid of tomorrow, for I have
seen yesterday and I love today.*
WILLIAM ALLEN WHITE

Sooner or later, we get there. Whether we consider
Bill Cosby fifty years old or fifty years young, the fact
remains that *Time Flies!*

Cosby, like millions of us, has reached that point
in middle life when, for better or for worse, he must
face the reality of growing old. He entertains and
perhaps even soothes us with amusing stories that
capture his reactions to the early, sobering signs of
the aging process. With the philosopher's sleight of
mind, he helps us understand that aging really isn't
that bad—or good!—that our state of mind about the
process is what's most important. We laugh along
with him as he gets on the mark and gets ready for

what promises to be a fruitful passage through the "golden years"; Bill Cosby will grow old, but he will never grow dim.

Throughout his career, Cosby has served as our puckish and empathic guide to humorous journeys through the fitful stages of childhood, adolescence, young adulthood, and parenthood. He is a perceptive social commentator whose comedy evolves from real-life dramas. We can identify our own experiences and reactions with many of his, and we don't mind that his humor, sometimes bittersweet, touches on the pain as well as the joy of our passage.

Time Flies offers Cosby a new and special challenge. He cheerfully peels away the layers of our normal defenses, allowing us to laugh at ourselves and at life's ups and downs. Unlike the earlier stages of development, growing old can be an especially poignant time, full of rewarding but difficult tasks. The "best years of our lives" are frequently marred by a slow but inevitable decline in our physical and, occasionally, mental abilities. Unfortunately, the gradual biological deterioration that accompanies our advanced years is often aggravated by society's negative myths about aging and lifestyles inhospitable to our well-being.

My own reactions to the early signs of aging

were, to some degree, the product of fears and misconceptions I absorbed while growing up American. I was not looking forward to a peaceful old age "on golden pond," and my mind-set was decidedly negative toward this twilight phase of life. I became a bit melancholy and, like Cosby, uneasy about reaching my Big Birthday. I declined a fiftieth birthday party because I felt that it was no cause for celebration. Did I want to keep my age a secret, perhaps hoping later to masquerade as a much younger person? My brain was not working rationally. I finally realized that I was experiencing an attack of aging anxiety, a non-Freudian entity that was more immediately worrisome than the fear of death itself.

Cosby and I—and possibly you—are having concerns that psychologists tell us are appropriate to our developmental stage in the life cycle. Many people in their forties and fifties become nervous about growing old before they experience the so-called mid-life crisis. Women at this stage worry about the approach of menopause, men about declining sexual performance, and both bemoan lives that could have been richer, fuller, or more successful. Many middle-aged people plunge into new careers, new interests, and new relationships as if this was their last chance to experiment with life before senility sets in. Fear of the stereotypes of old age is, I suspect, one of the critical ingredients in the mid-life crisis.

Even psychologists and psychiatrists are not immune to such feelings of panic. It is normal to experience a little anxiety and resistance toward some of the signposts along the road to growing old. For example, Cosby is very funny on the subject of his anxieties about trifocals; I ignored my need for bifocals for several years before yielding to the obvious necessity, waiting until I could hardly read any printed matter and was unable to decipher a menu in anything less than full light before giving in. People worry that bifocals will make them appear old. (In my opinion, bifocals may threaten some men more than sexual impotence does. Only a limited number of people are in the know if you are sexually dysfunctional, but everyone can see your bifocals and assume that you are going downhill.)

One friend's anxieties about failing eyesight did not revolve entirely around the desire to look young. As a doctor, he knew that he needed bifocals because the lenses in his eyes were becoming rigid and inflexible. Was this also happening to other parts of his body? Would he eventually—and all too soon—completely lose his vision? And would he develop cataracts prematurely? A simple thing like bifocals sent him into a tailspin and made him feel afraid and vulnerable about his future.

Other early signs of aging can push the middle-aged to wonder whether the time has come for them to develop an old-person identity—whatever that is. Similar disturbing associations occur when one's gum lines begin to recede and the prospect of dentures must be acknowledged. Hearing deficiencies associated with aging may also be denied even though corrective hearing aids are readily available. At mid-life, too many people discover for the first time that, even with exercise, they cannot quite flatten their bellies anymore—and the paunch they always thought they could banish is obviously there to stay.

As Cosby notes, the pull of gravity over time wins the battle. Many people in their forties and fifties are obsessed with their potential physical decline and fear that the time will quickly arrive when they require a wheelchair or are unable to rise from bed without assistance. Middle-aged people on the down slope often have these misgivings despite assurances from their physicians that they are in fine shape—for their age. It is hard for many of us to admit that we are no longer part of the Pepsi generation and that things don't get better with Coke.

I won't belabor the obvious and common personal apprehensions about gray hair and wrinkles. A youth-and-beauty-worshiping culture dominates America, where what is "new" is generally presumed to be better than what is "old." Yet the compulsion to look young and attractive is a burden that weighs much more heavily on women than on men. Women whose faces and figures were the primary elements of their identity and self-esteem may behave with particular desperation and denial when the aging process begins to show. They are the primary purchasers of "miracle" and "anti-aging" face creams and surgical face- and body-lifts as they try to hold back the tide of time. (And an increasing number of men are becoming clients of cosmetic surgeons.)

In my experience, some women develop aging anxiety as early as their thirties, particularly if they are concerned about conceiving children. For some, unfortunately, the onset of menopause can be a terminal symbol of lost youth and sex appeal. It would undoubtedly be a boon to older women if the attractiveness and allure of the "mature" woman were emphasized, with diminished focus on youth for its own sake. Progressive women are supporting such efforts on behalf of themselves and the elderly. However, as the middle-aged of both sexes grow older and older, they ultimately worry more about the health of their minds than the decline of their looks.

For example, a friend of my age, a lawyer, told me that her worst apprehensions about aging were evident whenever she read law quizzes in journals and had to struggle to remember the answers. She wondered whether she was losing her ability to think and recall information compared to when she was, say, twenty-five. Like others her age, she was not getting less intelligent; she was just getting less practice in taking tests. Contrary to popular notions, IQ does not decrease with age, although older people may follow logical sequences different from those of the young in their cognitive processes.

It is critical to recognize that learning ability does not necessarily disappear in those over sixty-five, or, indeed, over eighty. Many older, retired people return to school to earn college and graduate degrees. At any age, people can keep their brains functioning well by "exercising" them, by staying involved in intellectual pursuits, and by preserving a lively curiosity in the world around them. Disuse of the brain can lead to atrophy just as disuse of the body musculature can produce weakness and tissue wasting. An excellent way to nourish the intellect and maintain alertness is to stay involved with current affairs and politics, read newspapers and books, and tune to interesting radio and television programs. Stimulating the mind with fresh and challenging material helps keep it in shape.

Many people wonder whether memory loss is part of the natural aging process. It does seem that as we age we forget more easily, but the degree of the problem is greatly exaggerated and the causes are debatable. Sometimes older people appear to "forget" things because of memory overload or simple lack of interest. The so-called absentminded elderly may easily be distracted or appear withdrawn because their minds are on other things; often they can recall with perfect clarity events of decades past! Acute stress and anxiety may impair memory, just as they do in the young; but such impairment is more appropriately referred to as memory lapse rather than memory loss. Also, older people's memory sometimes appears to be slow because their reaction time is sluggish, but it is not necessarily lost.

Experts agree that the elderly are usually not "losing it," they are just not "using it" as often. Some of the perceived decline in their mental faculties results from the negative expectations of family, friends, and society—and from their own inaction.

Senior citizens might not be so concerned about

the decline in their mental faculties if it were not for a commonly held stereotype that our mental acuity deteriorates as we grow older. It's the old senility myth again. Cosby frequently jokes about our fears of losing our mental abilities. Unfortunately, the terror of senility sometimes becomes an overwhelming obsession of the aging.

Senility was once believed to be a condition that affected all older people at some point, but only a small percentage are afflicted, although the incidence increases significantly after the age of eighty-five. The most common form is Alzheimer's disease, which is a specific disease and not an inevitable consequence of the aging process. The causes of this dreaded mental deterioration have not been completely delineated, but in some cases the origin is a genetic abnormality.

Recent advances in the study of the brain have led researchers to believe that arteriosclerosis, hardening of the arteries of the brain, is not a cause of senility in and of itself, although it may lead to strokes and other brain dysfunctions. But arteriosclerosis is a disease that is more likely to affect individuals the longer they live. However, its development may be forestalled by a low-fat diet, good medical care for high blood pressure, and surgical techniques that clear blocked blood vessels. Other, currently experimental medical procedures may eventually lessen physical disruption of the brain. Impairment of brain function is not, of course, always related to organic causes. Some of the disorders mistaken for senility may arise from psychological conditions.

It is ironic that depression and worry can themselves create the appearance of senility in older people who do not experience its mental and physical deterioration. Depression occurs frequently in the aging population, but it is not a natural, or necessary, condition of that group. The elderly commonly suffer many losses—death of spouses, friends, even children; they frequently live in reduced or difficult circumstances and may endure physical disabilities that make them more liable to dismally low spirits. Psychological depression, characterized by withdrawal, sadness, and a lack of attention to personal needs and duties, is often wrongly perceived as dementia. When friends, family, and health care providers make this misdiagnosis the individual is frequently denied available treatment that could help to alleviate symptoms. Indeed, statistics show that the rate of suicide increases dramatically in the aged population. It is important, therefore, that friends and relatives learn to recognize signs of depression in the elderly before an avoidable tragedy occurs. Drugs and psychotherapy cannot remedy senility but can often restore health to those who suffer from melancholia and other behavioral symptoms.

It is a mystery to many scientists why the senility stereotype is so commonplace. Many people in their vintage years are actually smarter in many ways than they were at twenty-five or forty-five. Their experience and accumulated knowledge allows them to think, speak, and write with greater clarity. As we age, our judgment usually improves, giving us more intellectual balance and common sense. While the senility myth is, nonetheless, deep-seated in American culture, recent research and education have broadened our knowledge and enabled many of us to regard the old with greater objectivity.

New medical information and advances in scientific methods have ameliorated some of the disabilities that accompany aging and allowed many people to stay physically and mentally fit into their eighties and nineties. Modern science and medicine have changed both the concept of aging and treatment for the aged. New technology has produced refined surgical techniques to treat cataracts, orthopedic problems and joint disease, heart and cardiovascular disease, and dental problems. Smaller, more comfortable, and more effective hearing aids have greatly lessened the disability of hearing loss that plagues many older people. Partly as a response to these medical advances, the retirement age in most occupations has been raised to seventy or seventy-five, and in some fields there is no mandatory retirement at any age. Increasingly, the elderly are being judged by their ability to perform—which is as it should be—and not by some arbitrary cutoff age that defines the limits of their usefulness.

The importance of maintaining physical and mental fitness in middle-aged and older people is significant beyond the personal satisfaction and enhanced sense of well-being it produces. The social consequences are extraordinary as we witness the "graying" of America. Life expectancy in the United States is rising steadily, and the proportion of the population that is considered elderly has increased dramatically. At the turn of the twentieth century, women could expect to live to about the age of fifty-one and men forty-eight; today, those figures are nearly seventy-nine for women and seventy-one for men. (Rates for blacks and some other minorities are considerably lower because of physical and emotional conditions related to poverty and discrimination.) The approximately 28 million people in the

United States who are currently over sixty-five represent about 12 percent of the population. By the year 2030, more than 64 million Americans will be over sixty-five, comprising a staggering 20 percent of the population. Contrary to the popular misconception that most of the elderly are consigned to institutions, 95 percent live in the community, and most manage their own households.

Sociologists and demographers are, appropriately, beginning to write more frequently about the implications of these social trends. The fields of gerontology and geriatrics—both concerned with the scientific study of aging—have proliferated as social and medical scientists begin to grapple with the issues and problems of aging.

Growing old begins to concern most of us to some extent when we are in our fifties. But growing old *gracefully*, in good mental and physical health, is unnecessarily impeded by attitudes in our culture that devalue old age. Too often we accept the myths and stereotypes about aging that run counter to the common-sense observation that people, whether in late middle age or quite elderly, are still individuals —and as different from one another as young people are. Sometimes societal attitudes, more than actual diminution of our faculties, make it difficult for us to age comfortably.

Bill Cosby understands that older citizens face a prejudice called ageism, which can be as destructive and disabling as any other form of bigotry. Older people are often discriminated against in employment, education, and housing. Many are treated unfairly and even abused by younger members of the community, and sometimes by those within their own families. They are too commonly the butt of insulting and degrading ageist jokes. The stereotype that the elderly experience a second childhood has encouraged insensitive people to be patronizing and condescending. Gaining dignity and respect as whole persons is a challenge for the elderly; senior citizens themselves have organized to protest infantilization and the dissemination of myths and stereotypes. This is an "old is beautiful" movement, which all of us, young or old, should join; the life we embellish may be our own.

America's deep-rooted obsession with youth has metamorphosed the aging process into something akin to a fairy-tale beast, without the beauty, so that many flee from it in terror and disgust. Reminiscent of our childhood nightmares, the monster of old age drags us away as we cry out in vain for help; in the end, the creature devours us. We awake shaken, but relieved to discover that we are still alive—that we are still ourselves. When we are young, if we think about it at all, we expect immortality; we do not believe that old age and death can really happen to us. When we are older and presumably wiser, we should know better; but that is not always so.

Poets have suggested that death makes a mockery of us all, which is a jarring-enough thought. But pessimists have broadened this notion to suggest that getting older makes a mockery of us all, as well. That is like extending one's fear of the dark to include fear of the twilight. It is apparent that our fears, as we approach the twilight years, ultimately contribute to speeding our decline. In fact, many of us become what we are afraid we will become—or what society has told us we will become. Don't we all share at least some of the blame for making aging an evil force capable of poisoning the rest of our lives?

Growing old understandably reminds us that there is some chance that, in time, we will become debilitated, helpless, and dependent—a frightening thought. The fear of death is often not so much a fear of dying per se, but a dread of the complete loss of control over one's life and destiny. Similarly, apprehensions about aging often involve the terror of feeling abandoned and useless, rather than terror about aging itself. It is noteworthy that young people struggling for control over their lives frequently experience much more aging anxiety than the very old.

Happily for his readers, Cosby, in *Time Flies,* stares down the aging monster and mocks him right back: "Ha-ha to you, too!" Laughing at ourselves is never easy; it is even more difficult when we reach late middle age and perceive ourselves entering the ranks of the elderly. Some may feel that it is no joke to suffer diminished hearing, vision, and memory, that there is nothing funny about the threat of heart disease, stroke, and dementia. But, as Cosby demonstrates, a bit of counterphobia helps: the middle-aged and the elderly do benefit from a sense of humor about aging. The negative aspects of growing old have to be placed in perspective for the positive aspects to emerge.

Cosby teases us about skin creams, hair coloring, and cosmetic surgery, pointing out that they cannot stave off our ultimate decline forever, but he also knows that such assists to nature can help us feel more youthful and fit—and therefore in control—longer. For most people, aging need not and should not be a time of despair. Our sunset may lack some of the brightness of our sunrise, but it has its own special beauty if we learn to see and appreciate its possibilities. That is not always easy, yet one of the positive effects of this book is to encourage each of us to reflect on our own feelings about aging.

One indication that people's attitudes toward the elderly are changing is the vote of confidence Americans gave President Reagan in electing him to a second four-year term in 1984, when he was seventy-three years old. In addition to the trauma of a gunshot wound, he has survived surgical procedures for conditions common to the elderly. In 1987, President Reagan continues to function well mentally (whatever one may feel about his politics), despite his advancing age. Many other highly visible, energetic, and successful people are over the age of seventy: George Burns, Bob Hope, Lena Horne, Justice Thurgood Marshall, Mother Teresa, and Dr. Benjamin Spock, to name only a few.

Men and women over sixty-five who have an optimal aging attitude have managed to adapt positively to the triumphs and disappointments of life. Retired people are free of the pressures and strains of earning a living and getting ahead in the world; except for medical concerns, they should have a lot to feel good about. They have experienced and enjoyed living, and many have worked hard to raise a family.

In the mellowness of maturity, they have time for the leisurely pursuit of their own interests. Older people —at least some—can savor the wisdom that comes with age and come to terms with their Maker. It is a time in which the elderly can take a broad view of life across the generations and feel a sense of comradeship with all humankind.

If we fail to adapt well at this stage, then at the negative-attitude pole, life can be filled with disgust and despair. The elderly at this extreme are angry and contemptuous about all facets of life. Chronic disappointment contributes to this state of mind. Some, but not all, senior citizens are tipped toward the pole of despair by failing health and other disabilities. Many have medical problems that emerge after the wear and tear of time and prolonged exposure to health risks; about four out of five who are sixty-five and over have a chronic medical condition.

Physical weakness and persistent disability are among the most serious issues for the aged population. A rather strong connection between mind and body in the aged has been neglected: "A sound mind in a sound body" is ancient wisdom that needs reemphasis for seniors.

One of the most important ways in which the elderly can stay fit, physically and emotionally, is through regular exercise. Though their reflexes may have slowed and their stamina diminished, older people can keep their muscles and bodily organs functioning well by participating in physical activities like walking, swimming, bicycling, and other sports; conversely, the lack of exercise contributes to feeling old and tired. It is important, however, for all of them, particularly those who are impaired, to use moderation and respect the limitations of their bodies. They may not be able to exercise quite as vigorously as they once did—old bones break more easily and do not heal as well as they did in youth—but sensible, careful activity is both possible and desirable for most of the elderly. By slowing down a bit, the older person can savor each activity, a luxury most of us don't have when we're younger.

Researchers have also discovered that physical exercise reduces tension and improves function in the elderly, as it does in people of all ages. It is good prevention against the risks of depression and social withdrawal. Investigators further report that older people who remain active and exercise regularly perform better on tests of mental capacity. Senior citizens, in my opinion, must also have the opportunity to dance, sing, socialize, and just act silly on occasion.

Remaining sexually active is particularly important, for it provides good exercise as well as a strong, relaxing emotional release. Cosby jokes about his reduced libido when he discovers one gray pubic hair, but that problem is only in his head! Sexual energy may diminish in some people as they age, but the elderly should not succumb to that other great myth: that they are "over the hill" sexually. There is overwhelming evidence to suggest that the capacity for sexual performance and satisfaction exists well into the nineties. The chief causes of decreased sexual activity among senior citizens are physical disability, lack of interest, and, ironically, embarrassment that they *are* still interested. You can't always control physical limitations, but you can often control interest. Elderly men should not abstain from sex because of inhibiting stereotypes about "dirty old men." Elderly women who maintain strong sexual interests are also considered "odd." Their lives would surely be healthier if there were more "sexy senior citizens" around.

Part of any sexual enhancement and physical fitness program for the elderly should include good nutrition. Overweight, for example, speeds up any physical and sexual decline that accompanies aging. It also predisposes those of advanced years to be at high risk for diabetes, heart disease, stroke, and other disabilities. Poor nutrition and lack of essential vitamins and minerals can increase the odds of disease in bones, muscle, skin, internal organs, and even the brain.

Preparation for a healthy life during the vintage years should start when we are young. The early adoption of eating habits and regimens that support good health keeps us functioning well and longer into old age. Cigarette smoking, excessive alcohol and caffeine consumption, and the abuse of drugs, added to poor nutrition and lack of exercise, will make us look old far before our time. People who smoke, for instance, wrinkle more quickly. Those who overexpose themselves to the sun when they are young not only wrinkle faster, but increase their risk of skin cancer. Chronic stress and frustration will combine synergistically with all the other harmful activities to bring on premature aging.

Parents should begin early, through instruction and example, to prepare their youngsters for middle and old age by establishing healthy patterns that will serve them well in later life. They will then have less cause to restructure their habits in mid-life and beyond—the difficult process of "rebehaving" that Cosby humorously describes.

We can age more gracefully, but growing old is certainly not all bliss; aging eventually catches up with us. After age eighty-five, most of us will be restricted to some degree. Society can help by providing the necessary support services for the disabled elderly, namely, care by relatives, home care, supportive retirement communities, transportation access, and nursing homes. We must also try to lessen the burdens of poverty and expensive health care that increase the chances of severe stress and disability. Social Security and Medicare may have to expand their coverage to provide income and health insurance for the elderly, particularly those stricken with long-term and catastrophic illnesses.

When the time comes, older people should also have a right to die in a dignified fashion, without the needless prolongation of their lives by high-tech medical devices. The legal and ethical issues involved in unnecessarily maintaining the "living dead" are being debated by physicians, lawyers, clergy, and the elderly themselves.

As ever-increasing numbers of our population live longer, new attitudes and new discoveries have enabled society to take some of the "monster factor" out of aging. Perhaps Cosby and other middle-aged people will be able to look back one day and wonder,

"Why did I have all those anxieties when the early signs of aging crept up on me?"

One of the important messages Cosby conveys in this book is that the essential ingredients for a fulfilling life are the same for young and old. Older people need not undergo a prescribed disengagement from life. Love, friendship, a feeling of connectedness with others, and a sense of humor remain critical to our sense of well-being. As time goes by, we should not forget the redemptive power of smiling, laughing, and hugging.

Sooner or later, we will all get there—I hope in the right state of mind. But now let's go on to *Time Flies*.

Preface

WHERE TO, OLD COS?

I recently turned fifty, which is young for a tree, mid-life for an elephant, and ancient for a quarter-miler, whose son now says, "Dad, I just can't run the quarter with you anymore unless I bring something to read."

Fifty is a nice number for the states in the Union or for a national speed limit, but it is not a number that I was prepared to have hung on *me*. Fifty is supposed to be my *father's* age, but now Bill Cosby, *Junior,* is stuck with these elevated digits and everything they mean. A few days ago, a friend tried to cheer me up by saying, "Fifty is what forty used to be." He had made an inspirational point; and while I ponder it, my forty-year-old knees are suggesting I sit down and my forty-year-old eyes are looking for their glasses, whose location has been forgotten by my forty-year-old mind.

Am I over the hill? They keep telling me that the hill has been moved, that people are younger than ever. And I keep telling *them* that the high-jump bar has dropped from the six feet five I once easily cleared to the four feet nothing that is a Berlin wall for me now. It is not a pretty sight to see a man jumping a tennis net and going down like something snagged by a lobster fisherman.

"You're not getting older, you're getting better," says Dr. Joyce Brothers. This, however, is the kind of doctor who inspires a second opinion.

And so, as I approach the day when my tennis court jumping will be over the balls (or maybe the lines), I am moved to share some thoughts on aging with you, in case you happen to be getting older too. I am moved to reveal how aging feels to me—physically, mentally, and emotionally. Getting older, of course, is a distinctly better change than the one that brings you eulogies. In fact, a poet named Robert Browning considered it the best change of all:

> Grow old along with me!
> The best is yet to be.

On the days when I need aspirin to get out of bed, Browning is clearly a minor poet; but he was an optimist and there is always comfort in his lines, no matter how much you ache.

Whether or not Browning was right, most of my first fifty years have been golden ones. I have been an exceedingly lucky man, so I will settle for what is ahead being as good as what has gone by. I find myself moving toward what is ahead with a curious blend of both fighting and accepting the aging of Cosby, hoping that the philosopher was right when he said, "Old is always fifteen years from now."

Turning fifty has not bothered me, but people keep saying it *should* have, for fifty is one of those milestone ages that end in zero. Of course, in America *every* age ending in zero is considered a milestone age. Fifty is called The Big Five-O, but Forty is The Big Four-O and Thirty is The Big Three-O. A few months ago, my youngest daughter hit The Big One-O and she wasn't happy about it.

"I wish there were more single figures," she said.

Although reaching this half-century mark has not traumatized me, it *has* left me with disbelief about the flight of time. It seems that only yesterday I was fifteen and old people were people of forty, who were always going someplace to sit down. And now *I* am doing the sitting; and now my wife is telling me,

"You *sit* too much. You should get up and *do* something."

"Okay," I say, "let's have some sex."

"Just *sit* there."

When I was eight, an uncle said, "Bill, how long would you like to live?"

"A hundred million years," I replied.

"That's a ripe old age. I wonder what you'll *look* like at a hundred million."

"Oh, I'll just be me," I said.

Now, however, considerably short of the hundred-million mark, I am having to learn to accept a new me, one who has to drink skim milk, which looks like the wash for a paintbrush; one whose stomach refuses to process another jalapeño pepper; and one for whom a lobster is crustacean cyanide.

"If you want a lobster," my doctor says, "just eat the shell."

Have I *also* become just the shell? Well, in one or two places, the meat *is* missing. For example, I am now a man with the ability to dial a telephone number and, while the phone is ringing, forget whom he is calling. Just yesterday, I made such a blind call and a person answered with a voice I did not know. Like a burglar doing research, I quickly hung up, and then I thought about age.

Wiser men than I have thought about age and have never figured out anything to do except say, "Happy birthday." What, after all, *is* old? To a child of seven, ten is old; and to a child of ten, twenty-five is middle-aged and fifty is an archaeological exhibit. And to me, a man of seventy is . . . what I want to be, weighing 195, playing tennis with convalescents, and hearing well enough to hear one of my grandchildren sweetly say, "Grandpa, was 'The Cosby Show' anything like 'I Love Lucy'?"

1

FROM TEMPLE
TO TIRE RACK

If a Body Lose a Body

In the beginning, Temple was not just my college but a description of my body as well. And I was not just *any* temple but the Temple of Karnak. Like most young men, I was a perpetual motion machine. I would start playing basketball at eight o'clock in the morning, stop for lunch of a cupcake and Coke, play touch football all afternoon (on an asphalt field that makes AstroTurf seem like eiderdown), have a couple of steaks and a quart or two of milk for dinner, and then wonder if I could shake off the day's lethargy and find a pickup triathlon for the evening. In those years when I was immortal, I could eat a whole pizza on the run, never even pausing to taste it, and then my magnificent body would burn it as if it were merely cellophane.

"Chew your food!" my mother would say.

"Can't!" I would cry as if I'd just heard the starter's gun. "I don't have time!"

"You've *got* to chew your food. Why do you have *teeth?*"

"I don't know. Why?"

No mother or malady could stop me. Had I pulled a muscle in my groin? No problem: it would heal in an hour or two. Meanwhile, I could play without it. Had I separated my shoulder? It made no difference. Only softies needed shoulders that were attached.

I was physically such a splendid thing that one of my pastimes was pausing nude before mirrors—always in my own house, of course—to admire the 195 pounds of Super Cos. How I pitied all the men who weren't me, especially my father. Not only did he lack my flawless muscular definition, but he also had rolls of fat on both his sides that were known as "love handles," and he grunted whenever he sat down. He usually concealed these handles beneath a sport shirt that hung over his waist, but I knew they were there; and when I looked at him, I felt the grand arrogance of youth and I thought, *There is no way I will ever look like that.* I vowed that my only grunts would come when I crashed through for touchdowns, and I vowed that my no-frills frame would never be adorned by love handles or any other utensils.

Yes, when I was twenty-one, as Frank Sinatra likes to report, it was a very good year for full court games and quarter miles and 195 pounds of mozzarella-filled muscle. And even a few years later in that golden decade, when I was twenty-eight, the former Temple three-letter man was still high-jumping six feet five with the body that Michelangelo really had wanted when he'd had to settle for David.

But when I was thirty . . .

One day just after my thirtieth birthday, I was playing basketball with some teenage boys, trying not to be patronizing while I taught them some of my moves. Suddenly, while I was fighting for position under the backboard, one of the boys went up high for the ball. For a moment, I accompanied him and then I returned to the launching pad. A little while later, he also came down and found me pondering a melancholy truth: if a man of thirty wants to go flying with a boy of sixteen, he had better do it on Pan Am.

What had happened to the temple? It was being vandalized, and the vandal was time.

One morning the following year, after I had spent the previous day jogging, I woke up and wondered who had come into my bed and put a knife in my right thigh. There was, however, no pain in my left one: it was painlessly paralyzed.

A few days later, when I felt healed, I went jogging again and the pain returned, this time a knife in my knee. With a burst of machismo, I ignored it and continued to run.

What's the matter with you? said one of my legs. *Didn't you hear us when we first spoke to you? The legs go first, so we want to take this opportunity to say good-bye.*

A couple of weeks after that, I felt an ache in my shoulder when I began to brush my hair. Of all the indignities! A three-letter man going on the injured list during his toilette! A man who had laughed at losing his groin, a man who had *dared* his shoulder to separate, was being drawn into the world of liniments!

Moreover, the hair that I was trying to find the strength to brush, one of the fundamentals of my manliness, was being rearranged in ways both funny and sad. Instead of growing hair on my head, I now was growing it in places where I didn't need it, like the top of my ear. A strand had sprouted there overnight and made me look like something in *The Cat in the Hat.*

As I helplessly watched my body turn from a

temple to a storefront church, I was filled with frustration and disgust. I was in a war. Was it a war I *wanted?* I had no choice: I had been the victim of a sneak attack by an enemy called aging, an enemy that was daring me to play a game of beat the clock.

And so, I became a part-time athlete, desperately trying to recycle myself to a rough approximation of my former mint condition, desperately trying to keep my father's body from taking over mine. Sports that once had been effortless fun were now painful work as I tried to recapture vanishing skills and do what I once had done with such happy ease: to be as fast, as graceful, and as strong as I had been for my three varsities in 1956. Needless to say, the odds on my succeeding were almost as good as the odds on a bullfighter losing his ear to a bull.

I did not want to turn to playing golf because golf is about as much exercise as shuffling cards. Instead, I became a tennis player and I got pretty good. In fact, I am now considered to be one of the best celebrity players. Of course, this is not a Wimbledon group. Mother Teresa is a celebrity too.

These Jockeys Are Good
in the Stretch

During these twenty years of competing with time, I have been forced to witness many other signs of defeat deep in the hide of me, and on the top as well. It distresses me to report that, at the half, the score is: Time—37, Cosby—0. For the man of fifty, it is always third and long yardage, with a nearsighted quarterback.

All the assorted parts of me used to be flat and hard; but in these twenty years of going downhill, I have seen the growth of a gut, the thickening of thighs, the emergence of flab, the receding of a hairline, and the coming forth of gas. And the *most* mortifying betrayal of me by my flesh has been one particular form of the flab: the growth of love handles, which are hated handles now that they've moved from my father to me. A man needs rungs on his side only if someone is going to climb him.

Love handles are more than just depressing

breaks in a symmetry that women once joined me in admiring: they also destroy your lower abdominal chic because your Jockey shorts no longer fit; and it is a point of pride for the American male to keep the same size Jockey shorts for his entire life. He can lose his house in a crap game and his wife to the mailman, but his ego cannot tolerate an increase in his Jockey short size; and so, you have a man with a brand-new 40-inch waist who is trying to get into size 36 Jockey shorts, a man who is now wearing a combination of supporter and tourniquet. Proud men in their thirties and forties have gone to the brink of gangrene to maintain the interior fashion of their youth.

And this proud man of fifty has been on the brink of embarrassment, too. One day last week, I went to a men's store and asked for three pairs of Jockey shorts.

"What size, sir?" said the clerk.

"Thirty-four," I replied.

"Would you like them gift wrapped?" he said.

When I brought the Jockey shorts home, I cleverly cut slits in the sides of each pair so that there would be a chance for blood to flow below my waist.

Your pants are an even greater challenge once your stomach muscles have surrendered to fat because you cannot fake your belt size the way you can fake the size of your Jockey shorts. If you're a 38 waist, you might be able to fake the first hole of a 36 belt, but a 34 will circumnavigate you about as neatly as Columbus reached India.

No matter what size belt is strangling you, there are times when it will disappear under a roll of dough. This roll has a texture that feels like a melting candle. You can grab it with your fingers and even look under it to see if anything besides your belt is hiding there—a deck of cards, perhaps, or an overdue library book.

I wish that there were a way to take a shower and still keep on my clothes, for the sight of my naked body to me is like an X-rated film to an archbishop. I look down and I can see it all, the rolling hills of fat, and the view moves me to pray:

God, either give me longer arms or put my feet higher, perhaps at my knees, so I can take off my shoes without feeling as though I'm about to give birth.

Restoring the Navel Base

I once had a lovely body and vestiges of it still exist. I know, for example, that I once had pectoral muscles because the two brown dots that marked their location still remain on my chest. The first twenty or thirty times that a middle-aged man beholds such a vestigial body, he decides that beauty is in the eye of the beholder, and breaking down is in there too.

"It doesn't really look that bad," he says, an observation equivalent to the captain of the *Titanic* announcing, "We may be stopping near Newfoundland for a while." Living in this fantasy isn't easy for you because certain indications of your decline keep coming from other people, who look smilingly at your stomach and say such cute things as "Can you feel it kicking yet?"

However, once you have passed through your stage of denial—your lunatic stage—then you are ready to say, "Well, okay, I admit it. Maybe I *do* have a certain amount of flab, sag, and bloat, but I can get *rid* of it any time I want. I can exercise, I can diet, and there are wonderful new operations."

Your diet right now, of course, is chocolate cake and self-deception: you have convinced yourself that it would not be hard to find your navel again. In fact, you do catch sight of it from time to time. While you are standing, it's the same fine circle that was part of your charm at the beach; but when you sit down, your geometry changes and the navel turns from a circle into a slit. In fact, the navel of a man of fifty belongs on Dracula because it hides from the light.

It is also a tiny reservoir. One recent day, I got out of the shower, dried myself, and then accidentally knocked my toothbrush from the sink to the floor. When I bent down to pick it up, enough water came out of my navel to make a hydrangea bloom.

The restoration of a navel base may be more important to a belly dancer than to you, but such restoration is a symbolic part of your war on fat. After years of telling yourself that you don't really look that bad, the day finally arrives when you have to admit that the emperor has no clothes and parts of him look like the empress. And you also have to admit that the mound in your stomach that forms after a meal is now taking longer to disappear; it may even take years.

Moreover, as your size increases, your energy is going down. Like Noël Coward's mad Englishman, I used to play three sets of tennis that began at high noon; but now one set of doubles at four is fine—or one lively game of bridge—because I have to get ready for the main event. I have to get ready for dinner.

Because of my dedication to the main event, I was recently disheartened by a story that my ten-year-old daughter told me. Her teacher had somehow managed to inform the class that the only thing in an adult that keeps on growing is the nose; but the problem is that I have been doing no exercises for the nose—except, of course, inhaling new dinners.

"You know, Daddy, the teacher was wrong," my daughter then said.

"In what way, dear?" I asked her.

"Well, the stomach *also* grows. At least *yours* does."

Can You Dig It?

Whenever I see a picture of myself at twenty-three, I know that beneath all this superfluous flesh, there has got to be a body somewhere. And so, I have become an archaeologist digging in the ruins of myself, in the junkyard beneath my spare tire, to find the pure body below. I know that such archaeology cannot restore my hair or my old eyesight, and it cannot get me a new Achilles tendon or a new pair of lungs. All it can do is let me be reconciled with my old suits.

From time to time, I go into my closet and poignantly address what is hanging there.

"Suits," I say, "don't go anywhere. I'm coming back."

Once in a while, I *do* return; and, by happy coincidence, by the time that I do, the suit is back in style.

The man who is striving for a reconciliation with his old suits will be wise to pick only certain moments to look at himself. For example, he should not look at himself immediately after dinner because the food is still there and the spare tire is inflated to maximum pressure. The ideal time to look at yourself is first thing in the morning, when you are not fully awake.

Shake a Leg

One of the compensations of getting older (and so far, I've thought of only one) is that the medicine ball in your stomach forces you to replace the athletic skills you have lost with interesting new ones. For example, you learn the challenging gymnastic arts of putting on your socks and tying your shoes. Sock putting on and shoe tying are not yet AAU events, of course, but at times they are harder for me than it was to clear a high-jump bar at six feet seven.

When a man with an excess of midsectional bloat bends to tie his shoe, his reach is not only obstructed but he may even cut off his wind and find the blood rushing to his head. It is a dangerous part of getting dressed.

"Why is Daddy taking a nap on the floor?" your son says to your wife.

"Oh, he's not taking a nap," she replies. "He passed out."

"From drinking something?"

"No, he was trying to tie his shoe and that's not easy for a man of his age. He really should go to spring training before he tries it."

"I've got a good idea, Mommy!"

"What's that?"

"Let's fix it so Daddy doesn't have to *wear* shoes and then he'll be conscious much more."

"You mean move to the beach so he can go barefoot all the time?"

"No, let's get him some *slipper* socks."

"A nice thought, honey, but he can't put *those* on either."

This mother has obviously seen me in the morning. There have been times when I was so out of shape that I could have used the help of a small boy in putting on my socks. Without such a boy, I was able to put on my socks only by picking up each leg with both hands and then putting my heel on a chair.

Without such a boy *or* a chair, a man of my age who puts on a sock is participating in an event that requires split-second timing. As the Fernando Valenzuela of sock putting on, let me tell you how I do it. I raise my leg as high as I can; and then, for the second or two that my foot is quivering at its peak, I quickly bring the sock down over my toes. When my foot hits the floor, I finish pulling up the sock.

It is clear to me why "Miami Vice" has been so popular with men. Because millions of them watch it and dream of never again wearing socks.

Still another bit of sartorial aerobics for the middle-aged man is buttoning a dress shirt all the way up to the top before tying a tie. Because your neck has grown to keep pace with the rest of you, your top button prefers not to make the trip all the way to the buttonhole. In fact, the button below it is tight enough—and sometimes the one below that. What you need are dress shirts with zippers.

In your gritty effort to close the top button, you first lift your chin and then you begin to turn and bob your head. What you now are involved in is an original way to commit suicide because you are choking yourself: as you get the top button halfway into the hole, you feel you can't breathe and your face might explode. You wonder if the Heimlich maneuver has ever been used for a man getting dressed. Six or seven times, you bring the button to the hole and manage to get it halfway in while making little gurgling sounds, as if you are gargling without water.

Eventually, of course, your acrobatics end because the button snaps.

It is precisely what your mind was just about to do.

There is, of course, one other way for a man with a size 17 neck to fit into a 15 1/2 collar: with the help of one of his children. Sometimes, when I'm not in the mood for a long lonely struggle to squeeze into my shirt, I call one of my daughters and ask her to strangle me so I can close the button. She grabs the skin of my neck and pulls it tight, I button the button, and then she lets go and my neck expands. I now cannot swallow and have to take all my meals intravenously; and if the button ever snaps, it might kill a passerby; but I am a 15 1/2 again. After all, clothes make the man, even if the man is turning blue.

I've Got You Over My Skin

Some of the skin not far from what my daughter jams into my collar has lately started to develop little black dots.

"Look at this thing that just popped out," I said to my wife last night as I pointed to one of them. "What do you think it is?"

"A rerun of adolescence," she said, not wanting to tell me the truth: that it was age. "You've been eating too much junk food. Underneath that skin of yours are ten thousand Twinkies."

How sweet of her to comfort me with the thought of fifty-year-old zits.

"You know, at *your* age," she often says, "you should get your food from a health food store."

Because of this suggestion, I *have* made a few trips to health food stores, but I have always left empty-handed, not because of any defect in the supplies but in the *customers*. Did you ever see the people who shop in those places? They are pale, skinny people who shuffle around. They may live forever, but they look half dead.

In a *steak* house, however, you see robust, ruddy people. They are dying, of course, but they *look* terrific.

Although I just can't take the plunge into bean sprouts or alfalfa, one day I did put a few carrot sticks and celery stalks into a bag and I took a healthful walk in the park. After a while, I sat down on a bench beside an old man, who was both smoking and eating a chocolate bar, two serious violations of a longevity diet.

"Do you mind my asking how old you are?" I said.

"Ninety-two," he replied.

"Well, if you smoke and eat *that* stuff, you're gonna die."

He took a hard look at my carrots and celery, and then he said, *"You're* dead *already."*

2

THAT MAGICIAN, YOUR MIND

The Case of the Living Case

It might have been lucky if your mind *had* snapped while you were trying to button your shirt because then you would have been taken away to a place where you would have worn mostly bathrobes and pajamas. Moreover, when the mind of a middle-aged man is still in one working piece, it is in excellent shape to torture him. Mine has tortured *me* creatively. It has, in fact, given new meaning to the word "being in a fog."

When you reach my age, the fog makes your head seem like London at dawn. For example, one morning you start the old routine of packing your attaché case before leaving for work. On this particular morning, however, you also have two shirts that are going to the cleaner and a can of insect spray in case you're attacked by killer bees. And so, you pick up the fully packed attaché case, the two shirts, and the insect spray; and there you stand, a well-organized man of mature years, who is ready to meet the day.

But not *this* day, for suddenly you remember that you have forgotten to put something into the case: the smudge pot you always like to have handy in case you run into a friend with frozen orange trees. So you open the case, put the smudge pot inside, and close it; and then you pick up the two shirts, the insect spray, and the case—and you look down to discover that something that was inside the case is now *outside:* a letter from the Internal Revenue Service inviting you to the upcoming auction of your house.

Now you open the case again, put the letter back inside, and close it. You pick up the shirts and the insect spray and then you discover that your new Whiffle ball, which had been inside the case, is slowly rolling across the floor. You are the owner of an attaché case that belongs in a Stephen King movie. You do not, of course, need a piece of leather to destroy your mind because at your current age your mind can nicely self-destruct. Nonetheless, here is a case that somehow has been repacking itself.

After putting the Wiffle® ball back, you decide to get a drink of orange juice. What you really need is a cold beer, but you take the orange juice because you want to keep a clear head in your battle with your possessions. And so, you go to the refrigerator and pour out a glass of juice. While drinking it, you hope that the vitamins will go directly to your brain. Then you pick up the case, pick up the two shirts, and are on your way back to the front door when your refreshed brain says, "Just a minute, pal. What did you do with the insect spray?"

With growing despair, you begin a hunt for it. There is no point, of course, in also hunting for your mind: it is permanently lost. After a while, you drift back upstairs and are about to start the day again when your eye happens to fall on your desk, where is sitting the can of insect spray.

How did it get all the way up there? Why does the salmon swim upstream? Why is there a law against removing a mattress tag? Why do children always wait to ask you questions until you're on the phone? Why are the Atlanta Braves in the Western Division? Some cosmic questions can never be answered.

And now, ostensibly in control once again, you go back downstairs, pick up the attaché case, and cannot find the shirts. The reason you cannot find them is that you left them at the front door on your way back upstairs to look for the insect spray; but you cannot remember this right now because you have entered a period in which you cannot remember your name without looking in your wallet.

At this point, you decide it is getting late—both in the morning and in your life—and you will find the shirts tomorrow; so you go back to the front door, where the shirts are waiting for you, still neatly buttoned up. *You,* on the other hand, are not wrapped too tight.

One more time, you pick up the shirts, the attaché case, and then softly say to whatever puckish powers run the universe, "Now what the hell did I do with the insect spray?"

You're losing it, old boy, says your mind.

"You mean the insect spray?" you reply.

No, much more than that.

"Nonsense; I'm just tired."

Really? Then where is the spray?

"In the attaché case."

Okay, look, says your mind.

"I don't *have* to look; I know it's there," you

reply, continuing to talk to yourself without moving your lips.

You're afraid *to look.*

"No, I'm not."

And you open the case, try not to look inside, and you find the spray nestled mockingly there. You now decide to stop thinking about what you are carrying and go to work at once, hoping that you will not arrive at the office in your Jockey shorts.

Wait a minute . . . Did you remember to put them *on?*

And did you also remember that when you were young, you never dreamed that anything like this could happen to you? A young man has absolutely no notion that life will one day turn him into one of the Three Stooges.

When I was fifteen and arrogant—a redundancy, of course—I once heard some really old people in their forties telling each other how their minds were playing tricks on them.

What stupid people, I thought. *How can your mind play a* trick *on you? It's right there inside your* skull. *How can it whisper so you can't* hear *it?*

But now I know only too well that the mind of a man my age is a magician who could play Radio City.

Through a Glass Darkly

I wear glasses, primarily so I can look for the things that I keep losing. One day, however, I did something I do not usually do: I pushed the glasses up to the top of my head when I began to read a magazine because I do not need them for reading. A few minutes later, I put the magazine down, walked out of the office in my house, and went to the kitchen for a glass of lemonade. When I returned to the office, my children were circling my desk like vultures around a dying zebra.

"I would like all of you to please leave Daddy's stuff alone," I told them.

"Don't mind us, Daddy," said my little one. "We're just playing."

"And this is the one place I don't *want* you to play."

"What's this, Daddy?" she said, picking up a script she was planning to shred.

"Your next fifty meals," I replied. "Now go outside and bother your mother. That's what mothers are for."

After they had left, I went back to my reading; but a few minutes later, I decided that I wanted to go to town for some shopping; and so, I put on my jacket, and I also wanted to put on my glasses to drive because part of safe driving is being able to see the other cars.

But where *were* my glasses?

I began to look around my desk, both in and under things, wondering where my glasses had gone to hide. I checked my cigar humidor and I even checked the big box containing all the things I never use and cannot throw away. The reason I cannot throw them away is simple: some day a friend may call and say, "Do you happen to have any dried-up felt markers? I can't seem to find any in the stores. And do you also happen to have a two-inch pencil with the eraser chewed off? It's my favorite kind."

With a blend of determination and dismay, I now got up and started to walk around the office. I looked like a man who was hunting for Easter eggs.

This does it, I finally thought. *There's no question about it: the kids have definitely taken my glasses. Maybe they need them for the school play. Or maybe they think I'm handsomer without them.*

I did not, however, want to go right in and yell at the kids because such anger in the past had usually triggered the reply, "Of *course* you can't find something. You always leave your stuff lying all *over* the place. The other day there was a can of *insect* spray in the fridge. It had to be yours."

"If people would just leave my stuff where I *put* it," I always say with partial conviction.

I am just like any typical nuclear physicist. My office may look messy, but I know where every atom is.

After brooding about the situation for another few minutes, I suddenly decided that the culprit was not one of my children but my *wife,* who had moved my glasses to a place in our home where they made a better blend with the color scheme. However, greater than my anger at my wife was my desire to do my shopping in town; and so, in one last desperate effort, I searched the living room, the dining room, the kitchen, and even the fuse box.

At last, I went upstairs and searched the bedroom, after which I decided to go into the bathroom for five or ten aspirin. As I entered the bathroom, I caught sight of myself in the mirror; and I also caught sight of something on top of my head: my glasses.

They had been resting all this time on the great empty spaces there.

Three for the Show

Those glasses were trifocals, which were invented by Benjamin Franklin, who should have stuck to inventing things like electricity and the United States. Trifocals are given to many people my age who need three different fields of vision.

"These will be perfect for you, Mr. Cosby," said my ophthalmologist when he fitted me for my first pair. "In the top band of the glasses, you can see things far away. In the middle band, you can see things about fifty yards away. And in the bottom one, you can read your medicine."

In spite of the brilliance of Benjamin Franklin and your ophthalmologist, your first pair of trifocals can turn a simple stroll down the street into the asphalt equivalent of a trip up Mount Everest.

The adventure begins when you go for the knob of the door of the room you are trying to leave. You have left thousands of rooms before, so this particular departure should not be difficult. All you have to do is figure out how far away the doorknob is. In one lens of your glasses, it's two hundred feet; in another lens, it's on top of you; and in the third lens, it's missing. In the spirit of Magellan, you decide to determine the distance by a kind of ophthalmological navigation: you take the average of the two distances and conclude that the doorknob is one hundred feet away, give or take fifty feet. Unfortunately, the chart in your eye doctor's office was full of useless things like letters instead of doorknobs and elevator buttons.

Yes, elevator buttons. Approaching the elevator, you again have your choice of three lenses and three distances. Is the button thirty yards away, forty feet, or almost behind you? With one chance in three of being right, you quickly take your shot and you lose by jamming your index finger. You finally start to understand why people in their seventies and eighties who wear trifocals walk the way they do: with tiny steps. The problem is not in their legs. They simply do not want to walk off the edge of the cliff.

Many people my age, of course, do not want all the confusion that trifocals bring and prefer instead to go through life using three different pairs of glasses: one pair for reading, one pair for middle distance, and one pair for lunar eclipses. The flaw in this system, however, is that occasionally someone enters a room while you are between glasses and you are caught with your naked eyes. You are frozen in a moment when you are unable to put on a pair of your glasses, primarily because you don't know where they are; and so, you have to play an increasingly popular American game called Who the Hell Is That?

"Hi . . . George," you tentatively say, taking an educated guess that what you are seeing is not a woman.

And when a female voice replies, "Hi, Bill," you have new insight into the meaning of middle age.

While coping with middle age, at least I have the comfort of knowing that I will never have to cope with senility.

"Don't worry about senility," my grandfather used to say. "When it hits you, you won't know it."

And he was right. He lived to be ninety-eight years old, thinking for the last fifteen of them that he was Frederick Douglass.

Sights for Sore Eyes

The indoor adventures that trifocals lead you into are scary enough, but going outside with them adds new dimension to the terror. The first time I went outside with my new trifocals, I took a three-mile walk through the lobby of my ophthalmologist's building, climbed a five-foot curb, and then met an autograph-seeker who happened to be a giant eye.

"Mr. Cosby, could I have your autograph for my daughter?" said the eye.

"Yes, yes!" I replied. "Just don't eat me!"

After signing my name, I staggered on, expecting to encounter a sea monster at the traffic light; but instead, an enormous eyebrow came over and said, "Are you all right?"

"Would you please take me to a phone?" I told the eyebrow. "I want to call my wife."

When I reached the phone, I dug out some change and spent a few minutes trying to find the hole for it. Luckily I had enough change for the three wrong numbers I reached before I finally reached my own.

"Dear," I said to my wife, "this may be the last time you ever hear my voice, unless you come and get me before I'm run over. These trifocals are about to get me killed."

"You idiot," she tenderly said. "Take off the glasses and come home."

Memory Is Made of This

The poet T. S. Eliot said:

> April is the cruellest month . . .
> Mixing memory and desire.

Well, what I desire is my old memory, and not just in April; I forget messages in October, phone numbers in March, and assorted appointments in July. I do, of course, remember certain things. I remember my anniversary because it celebrates the happiest association of my life, an association with the person who knows how to save me from an intersection; and I remember my wife's birthday because she announces it well in advance and momentously, the way astronomers announce Halley's Comet. However, in a few dozen other endeavors, my memory can hardly be used as proof of man's evolution from the chimpanzees.

Short-term memory is particularly challenging. These days, whenever I come into a room, I need all my skill as a performer to pretend I remember why I came.

"Retrace your steps and it'll come to you," one of my children will say, for you can never fool your own children.

"Retrace them to *where?*" I reply.

Certain connections just seem to be beyond me at this age. For example, if someone calls me on the telephone and says, "Can you meet me at the Seven-Eleven at eight?" I show up at the Five-and-Ten at nine.

I used to be brilliant at remembering telephone numbers: I carried in my head more than fifty of them, complete with area codes, and some were even overseas. In those days, if you had said to me, "Bill, do you happen to know the number of the Yokohama Holiday Inn?" I would have given it to you at once, and I might even have thrown in the address and zip code. But today my mind is functioning in a different gear; in fact, it's not really a gear, it's neutral.

The telephone rings at our house and I pick up the receiver and say, "Hello." That much I still remember.

"Hello," a girl says, "is Erika there?"

"No, she isn't," I reply, still on top of things.

"Well, when she comes in, will you please tell her that Lori called?"

"I certainly will."

Lori's request is a simple one; a child of four can do it. And I should *get* a child of four because this man of fifty is not equal to the job.

But what a *proud* airhead I am! Someone will call on the phone and give me an important piece of information that must be preserved. Instead of writing it down, I decide to keep it in my head, perhaps because of all the room for it there.

"Write it down," says my wife.

Oh, you *don't have to write it down*, my ego tells me. *You can remember* that.

"Remember *what?*" I reply.

Do not, however, think that I am incapable of growth. After having forgotten an impressive number of messages, I finally started to write things down.

Okay, said my ego, *we're giving in a bit. But if we have to write things down, we certainly don't have to write them down in* longhand. *We can use a code, just like a doctor.*

And so, I began to write my reminders in code. For example:

Tell E that L called

The only problem was that when I tried to read the messages back, I needed some help from the CIA. Who was E? Who was L? Perhaps this message meant:

Tell Ennis that Linus called

Or perhaps:

Tell Ennis that London called

Or perhaps:

Tell the Extraterrestrials that
London called

Not only did I have trouble breaking the code, but sometimes I didn't recognize the handwriting. Who, I wondered, had become my pen pal?

As another part of this unintelligible correspondence with myself, I also keep a pad by the side of my bed for writing down great thoughts at night without having to turn on the light. In the morning, these great thoughts sound like excerpts from the Dead Sea Scrolls. The other day, for example, I awoke to read:

> Brans der grimble dbl wing &
> wang

Was this my solution to the mystery of life? Or a reminder to pick up cottage cheese?

I Wonder as I Wander

People above a certain age should not be allowed to have two cars unless they are identical because these people often have trouble remembering which car they happen to have brought with them. There are few moments in life more damaging to your self-esteem than to leave a football game, a supermarket, or a mall and forget not only where you left your car but where you left your mind because you cannot remember which car it *was*.

And so, you start to wander around in the wilderness, trying to conceal that you are looking for a car whose make has become foreign to you; it's on the tip of your mind, that pointy little place. Just as in looking for your glasses, you have to conceal that you are looking for something you handle every day; and a car, of course, is generally harder to misplace than glasses, especially a four-door.

When you parked the car, you had said to your mind, "Okay, now take this down: we're a blue Valiant parked in A2."

And your mind had replied, *Got it. Have fun shopping.*

So off you went, even walking backward part of the way to remember exactly how your car looked and exactly where it was.

For the next few minutes or hours, you keep interrupting your shopping to reassure yourself that nothing is simpler to remember than A2 blue Valiant. You even make up a little poem to fix the picture in your mind:

> Roses are red,
> My Valiant is blue.

An A1 car
In row A2.

When you leave the mall, however, you find that this verse has taken wings and in its place is a less-winged one:

Roses are red,
My car must be near.
Am I insured
For losing it here?

People like me need a cute little yellow sign in the back window of their cars:

NOBODY
ON
BOARD

The Face Is Familiar

That magician, my mind, can do another trick as impressive as losing my car: it can suddenly erase the name of a person that I not only know well but also happen to be looking at. I still cannot understand how I manage to do this trick, but I am capable of forgetting the name of someone I have known for years—for example, my wife.

I will walk up to a group of people who have never met Camille, proudly put my arm around her, and say, "This is my wife . . . my wife . . ."

And she will have to fill in the blank. Of course, the blank that cannot be filled is the one she married.

Even rehearsing her name doesn't help me. When I approach a group of people, my brain says, *Don't forget the name of your wife.*

And I reply, "Now how could I forget what's-her-name?"

But my wife should never laugh at me for my journeys into the fog. She is younger than I am, but she is already in training to be middle-aged: she is starting to have moments of wondering if she has put the right letter inside an envelope she has just sealed; and once a person starts wondering what she has put into an envelope just a moment before, it is only a short step to wondering if her return address is correct.

Losing track of the inside of an envelope is one thing, and losing track of your car is another, but at my age it is also possible to lose track of your *house.* It happens like this: you are talking on the phone to a person you haven't seen for years and you are describing the appeal of your house.

"It's a wonderful place," you say. "You really should come and see it."

"I'd love to," the other person says. "What's your address?"

And you reply, "Five sixty-one North Twenty-first Street," which is a lovely address but does not happen to be yours. You have given your old address, where you haven't lived for seven years. Your mind, like a French post office, now has trouble forwarding things.

Because of this condition, I am always sure to carry my wallet; and then, when a person requests my address, I can say, "Just a minute; it's right here on my license."

My name is there too, in case I am having a particularly bad day.

A Room with a View
of the Funny Farm

Although I like to work out on a track, I cover just as much ground inside my own house because, as I have confessed, I am constantly walking into a room, forgetting why I made the trip, and then trying to jog my memory by retracing my steps. Of all my short-term memory lapses, this one and forgetting my parking place are the two that at least can lead to some good because they lead to exercise.

With an object I need in mind, I take a short walk to a nearby room; but when I enter the room, I have forgotten what I came for. My body, however, still senses there must have been a point in making this trip.

We're here, says my body. *Pick it up.*

Pick up what? replies my mind.

As I begin to circle the room with big blank eyes, my mind stops talking to my body and addresses what's left of me, which isn't much.

You need a break, says my mind. *Stop circling the room and take a lap around the house.*

"No," I reply. "Before I take a lap, I'll stay in the room and look around. Maybe I'll find what I came in for."

Face it, old boy, says my mind. *You're starting to lose it.*

"Lose *what?* Is there something *else* I should be looking for?"

Eventually, I remember why I came, but only after returning to the other room and sitting down. I remember because the thought that left my mind went and hid in my behind and sitting down has jogged it loose. You can save yourself a lot of this traveling if you simply slap yourself on the behind whenever you start circling in search of a phantom pickup. Do not, of course, let your children see you dislodging the thought this way. They already suspect that certain things in you are rolling around loose.

Atten-shun!

All the failures of memory that can plague you, such as losing your car at a mall or losing your glasses on your forehead or losing the reason you entered a room, are minor when compared to the most embarrassing trick your mind can play: forgetting what you have been talking about. After scientists find a cure for the common cold, they will have to move on to a greater medical challenge: why a man my age clearly remembers events of thirty years ago but not what he said in the last thirty seconds. It is perhaps the most demoralizing moment that a middle-aged man can know, even worse than learning that his twenty-six-year-old son is about to move back into the house or that his high school sweetheart has applied for membership in the Gray Panthers.

The moment happens to you like this. You and another friend in his fifties are sitting together, perhaps at a party where none of the younger people will talk to you because you still read books, or perhaps in the waiting room of a doctor who specializes in the treatment of people who have begun to click. You have started talking to this man about a subject in which you always have been deeply interested: the history of hot chocolate. You can see that your friend is listening with attention as you spellbindingly reveal how the ancient South Americans invented hot chocolate for an après-sacrifice: they would toss a fellow tribesman into a volcano and then relax with a nice hot cup. Not only are you being fascinating, but you are also building to a major medical point: that hot chocolate is the safest drug and should be given to babies before they develop a yen for something else.

And so, you are merrily spinning these unforgettable thoughts, while your friend is responding with continuous support:

"Oh yes, Bill, absolutely . . . A point well taken and I'm taking it well . . . You've a wingéd tongue there, man . . . For sure, Bill, for sure . . ."

But suddenly another person approaches you and says, "Would either of you gentlemen like some coffee?"

"No, thank you," you reply.

"No coffee for me," says your friend.

"Some tea or prune juice, perhaps?"

"No, thanks."

"None for me."

"Perhaps a mint or a Tootsie Roll?"

"No, nothing, thanks."

"Right, nothing for me either."

And then you speak the chilling words: "Now where was I?"

You are trying to return to your train of thought and discover that you can't even find the station. And neither can your *friend,* who has been listening with such attention.

I have helplessly watched my mind shift into neutral on both sides of this grand embarrassment: as both the derailed storyteller and the lost listener. If you're the listener, you say to yourself:

He must think I haven't been listening, but I really have. *I* love *stories about . . . about . . . about . . . whatever he was saying.*

And if you're the storyteller, your distress is even more painful because your thoughts had been organized and you had been building to a point. You know many pointless stories, but this did not happen to be one. And so, seized by a mental power failure, the storyteller doubles back desperately in his memory, but he still cannot find the train of thought, which is running on a holiday schedule.

This is the general style of going blank one-on-one. If, however, the storyteller has been talking to more than one listener when he goes blank, then he has a chance to take a poll to reveal the subject he has been talking about.

"Listen, folks," he says, hoping that he is still concealing his dismay, "I never like to repeat myself, so please tell me if any of you has heard this story I was telling about . . . about . . ."

And hopefully he waits for someone to play Password with him.

But no one is able to play. At last, his mounting frustration makes him shed his subtlety and he says with a casual air, "By the way, does anyone here happen to remember what the hell I was talking about?"

"I'm afraid I don't," one listener will reply. "It happened too recently. But ask me about the night we put the donkey in the dean's office to celebrate Kennedy's election. Or ask me about the Battle of Gettysburg. Eighteen sixty-three is like yesterday to me."

"I can't remember it either," another listener will say, "but it was certainly memorable."

"Wait a minute now . . . it's coming to me," a

third will say. "Yes, here it *comes*. Chalk . . . chalk
. . . You were talking about the history of *chalk*."

The lesson for us middle-agers in this piteous tale
is clear: we cannot start a monologue leading to any
kind of punch line or point unless we are in an environment where no interruptions are possible. The
good environments for storytelling, like the confes-
sional, you can figure out for yourself; but even in the
ideal environment, people with sometime memories
like mine should still tell only the shortest possible
stories.

"Knock, knock," I said to my wife last night as
we settled down to some sophisticated after-dinner
talk.

"Who's there?" she replied, and I quickly moved
my story to its sparkling conclusion.

If, however, my "Knock, knock" had been followed by a phone call from one of my children re-
questing money by Federal Express, the story would
have been no easier to remember than my story of
why those old South Americans got acne.

No matter what the length of your discourse
happens to be, it is wise to carry a pencil and pad; and
then, when someone interrupts, you can say "Just a
second" and write down exactly where you stopped.

Of course, some people need more than a pad. Some people need cue cards.

The only good thing about the decline of my memory is that it has brought me closer to my mother, for she and I now forget everything at the same time. When I was younger, I used to look at my mother impatiently and think, *Lord, can't she remember anything?* But now that we go blank simultaneously, I look at her and think, *Is she supposed to say "Knock, knock" or am I?*

3

COULD I HAVE A SECOND OPINION?

Hello, Sponge

It is probably a good idea for a man in his middle years to get his annual physical from Dr. J because Dr. J would never tell him, "Things are getting spongy." This has become the favorite word of the American doctor in summing up the condition of a man my age. Whether he is referring to your prostate or your spine, "spongy" is what he calls it. You seem to be approaching the time when your entire body will be fit for mopping a floor.

"At least my lungs, they're *supposed* to be spongy, right?" you say to the doctor with a quietly desperate look in your eyes.

"No, your lungs are getting *hard*," he replies. "You're in what I like to call 'parts reversal': some of the things that are supposed to be hard are getting soft and some of the things that are supposed to be soft are getting hard. Your head, however, is still both."

"Doctor, is there anything I can *do* about the sponginess?" you ask.

"I'm afraid not," he smilingly says.

"What about the hardness?"

"Absolutely nothing, so just don't give it another thought. You know the way the generator light on the dashboard of your car sometimes goes on and you ignore it?"

"Yes."

"Well, ignore this too."

The doctor has been profoundly comforting with his generator analogy; you may as well get your next physical at a Texaco station. He does, of course, give you *some* advice.

"You have to cut down," he tells you.

"Cut down to what?" you say.

"Are you eating food?"

"Yes."

"Well, cut down, especially the stuff that has taste. Stop eating salt, sugar, egg yolks, red meat, whole milk, and almost everything else. Try to build your meals around parsley—but with no barbecue sauce, of course."

"Is chicken okay?" you ask him.

"Yes, but without the skin."

"It doesn't look good that way."

"Then close your eyes and add lemon juice."

At this age, you find that lemon juice has become the all-purpose seasoning: you squeeze it over the fish you have cooked with no salt and the chicken you have cooked with no oil and the eggs you have cooked with no yolks. Eating egg whites, of course, is the gastronomic equivalent of the tree that falls in the forest with no one there to hear it. Not only do egg whites have no taste, but their validity as food is somewhere between celery and cellophane.

Were it not for lemon juice, you might not even know when you were eating because tastelessness has become the heart of your cuisine: you sit down to heaping plates of celery and radishes, of cauliflower and boiled beets, of broccoli and watercress. I dare any scientist to discover what celery tastes like. Not only does your mouth not water at the sight of celery, it dries up; and so, the lemon juice is needed as a lubricant, too. Eating such a meal is almost as much fun as dining intravenously.

Good-bye, Jack Armstrong

"Eat your spinach and drink your milk."

When I was a boy in Philadelphia in the innocent Forties, this was the mealtime litany chanted by millions of mothers, who passionately believed in learning nutrition from cartoons. Popeye, the world's most able-bodied seaman, sent cans of spinach directly to his arms; and Jack Armstrong, the All-American Boy, sent glasses of milk directly to his knuckles and teeth. Of course, Popeye had an IQ of twelve and Jack Armstrong was still in high school at twenty, but they were the world's *healthiest* nitwits.

In the years that I was growing up, I began each day with a glass of milk, the perfect food, and a bowl of cereal that was covered by more of this perfection; and sometimes I also had bacon and eggs, the stuff of rural wholesomeness. For lunch (if I had time for it during my marathon of street play), I drank a whole *quart* of milk, sometimes so fast that I got a headache across one eye; and for dinner, I simply ate two steaks, which I didn't even bother to chew.

By feeding me like this, my mother had no doubt that I would live to one hundred and five, belting bullies all the way while also defending the flag.

And then I learned about cholesterol.

"Did I hear you say that you eat fried egg sandwiches?" my doctor asked me one day when I was in my forties.

"With a pickle," I replied.

"You'd be better off eating cyanide; it has less cholesterol."

"But doctor, I still feel in pretty good *shape*. My body is still a *temple*."

"No, it's not: it's Fat City."

And so, from that moment on, whenever I had eggs, I ate only the whites. To compensate for the loss of the yolks, I quadrupled my intake of spinach—and it made me sick. Popeye is undoubtedly in a naval hospital right now, wondering why all our mothers tried to poison us.

Lead Us Not into McDonald's

Unsure of what to put into my mouth besides a cigar, I now go wandering through the culinary minefields of America, trying to avoid the steps that might be lethal. You will pardon the mixed metaphor—at fifty, I cannot keep both my appointments and my metaphors straight—but these minefields are constantly calling to me:

Come, clog your arteries at Wendy's!
Come, set up your bypass at Burger King!
Come, get your Kentucky Fried triglycerides!
Come, meet your maker at Bar-B-Q!

The temptations are international, for the Chinese are also trying to turn off my circulation. Oh, for the days when MSG meant only Madison Square Garden! At times, of course, I cannot resist the call of the Chinese restaurant; but at such times, I have to turn away from everything succulent and say to the waiter, "Just bring me a menu from the Long March."

Even such a seemingly harmless dish as French toast has now become tasty Russian roulette. Because this game is too dangerous for me, I have to say to waiters, "I'd like an order of French toast, but hold the bread. And if you can figure out what French toast without the bread looks like, then don't use any eggs or milk in the batter, and no butter in the frying, please."

What I want is a plate of maple syrup—from which the sugar has been removed. And I also want maple syrup on my lettuce, cauliflower, celery, parsley, and boiled beets so that I will be able to know when I am eating. I *used* to know when I was eating because I tasted the food going down, but those were the days before I learned that my arteries were approaching gridlock. Those were the days before I was told to switch from soft drinks to distilled water, as if I were not a person but a battery. And those were the days before I was constantly hungry, before I began to fear that my body would soon start feeding on itself and go for the reddest meat around: my heart.

It is a constant strain on you to be eating like this. You find yourself picking up such things as a box of toasted Swedish thins, which make a sound in your teeth but cause no response in your stomach. No wonder so many Swedes are depressed.

I want potato chips with salt! says your mouth. *I want potato chips with salt from the* Dead Sea! *How dearly I would love them!*

But you also love life, so you settle for the leafy vegetables, which act as diuretics. There is, however, one compensation in this boring new diet of leafy diuretics: your urine is clearer than it ever has been. You were, of course, happier in the days when your head was clear and your urine wasn't, but a man of fifty has to accept his fog wherever it forms—and he has to look ahead with hope. *My* hope comes from seeing all the people in their seventies who are feasting on triglycerides. When I recently took an ocean cruise, I noticed that my mother, my in-laws, and many of their contemporaries ate no more than six times a day, and they did not eat parsley or sunflower seeds. And so, I look forward to surviving my sixties and then merrily returning to the food that poisoned Jack Armstrong.

The first thing I'm going to do when I turn seventy is go to a restaurant like the one across the street from the Mayo Clinic, which is a feeder system for the Clinic. When I had my physical at Mayo, I dropped into this restaurant and discovered that it probably holds the original patent on cholesterol: everything in sight was covered with chocolate, sugar, fat, or grease. They might as well have served you a plate of corks for your arteries.

Well, that's where I'm going when I hit seventy and can return to deadly deliciousness. I'll take a seat at a table there and smilingly summon the waitress.

"Miss," I'll say, "are your triglycerides fresh?"

"Oh, they certainly are."

"And does the chef have a good touch with fatty molecules?"

"Oh, yes."

"Excellent. Bring me a plate of bacon and egg yolks, with side orders of sausages and crullers. And fry it all in axle grease."

Let's Make a Deal

Until I reach these happy seventies, I will have to learn what I call "rebehaving," which means resisting the temptation of food that waters instead of dries my mouth. I will have to walk past cheeseburgers, cheesecake, and hoagies the way that Ray Milland walked past saloons in *The Lost Weekend*. Of course, I am losing more than just a weekend: I am losing good food for the next twenty years—about twenty-two thousand meals. It is wonderful training if you are planning to forget the shore next summer and take your vacation in a gulag.

And so, I now yearn for just one pancake with a dab of butter, but I have to settle for bean sprouts, wheat germ, tofu, and other things almost as tasty as library paste. I wander like a lost soul past Burger King and Bar-B-Q, pathetically trying to negotiate with myself:

"Listen, I've been good for so long. Couldn't I have just *one*—"

Do you want to live long enough to see your children leave the house?

"But just *one* bagel with the egg whites at lunch. Have mercy! Those egg whites are so boring that I'm falling *asleep*. I'm liable to *choke*."

There's butter, salt, and sugar in that bagel.

"I'll toast it and burn that stuff off."

You'll toast the whole wheat bread for your cucumber sandwich.

"If you let me have the bagel, I promise I'll do *four* extra laps on the track."

You want them to find all that cholesterol in the autopsy? We want your autopsy to look good.

"Okay, forget the bagel. How about just one buttermilk pancake?"

Buttermilk pancake? Those things are swallowed by spies who don't want to be captured alive!

Because I am trying to rebehave, I occasionally spend a week drinking an herbal cocktail every night at bedtime. This particular brew is made by boiling water with assorted roots and herbs that look as though they have been harvested from the inside of a vacuum cleaner bag. And while it boils, its aroma drifts through the house, decreasing its value and moving my wife to look up the number of the Environmental Protection Agency. The purpose of this drink is to clean out my clogged arteries; but Drano would also work and it would certainly taste better.

Women and Children Last

From time to time these days, either my wife or one of my children will sweetly say to me, "We want to keep you around a long time."

I do not mind this sentiment coming from a

creditor, but when it comes from a loved one, I feel a curious blend of depression, anger, and gratitude. I am happy that the members of my family are eager for me to become an antique, but why do they think that *I* will go first? Just because I moan for a couple of days after playing anything livelier than pre-dinner doubles? After all, I am only at midlife; and if fifty is midlife, then I will live to be a hundred, when my quarter miles will be timed not with watches but with calendars.

Although their saying "We want to keep you around a long time" does indicate that they love me, it also indicates that they are keeping themselves free for my memorial service. However, I need not be reminded by them about the way of all flesh. Like everyone else who makes the mistake of getting older, I begin each day with coffee and obituaries. I open the morning paper, turn to the obituary page, and nervously check out the ages of those who've checked out, hoping to discover that all of them were at least a hundred. I do not mind, of course, if a few of them were ninety-five; but when I find ages close to mine, I get a chill in my aching bones and I search for comfort in the cause of the death. What I don't want to find is a heart attack on a tennis court, in a French restaurant, or while attending a Temple reunion. I want to find death from a firing squad or from an attack by soldier ants or from accidentally going over Niagara Falls.

The Numbers Game

In addition to telling me that they want to keep me around a long time, my children also like to cheer me up by saying, "You look good, Dad." Strangely enough, the older I get, the more often I look good; and therefore my handsomeness will reach its peak when they bury me.

Precisely what do my children *mean* by telling me that I look good? Good compared to *what?* The people in intensive care? When she turned fifty, Gloria Steinem said, "This is what fifty looks like," so I simply look my age.

I may have made a mistake in this book by giving my real age, but I couldn't help it: this is the most age-conscious nation in the world and I was just being a real American. In fact, a man of fifty is suddenly aware that no story written about Americans can exist without those two little numbers following our names. And they follow our names for no reason; it would make more sense if those numbers were our IQs. For example:

> Sam Russell, 52, said today that he cannot balance either his checkbook or his mind.

This is a typical line in an American newspaper; but the routine usage of Sam's age gives us no insight into the cause of his bewilderment. If, however, the numbers were his *IQ*, they would be more revealing:

> Sam Russell, 83, said today that he cannot balance either his checkbook or his mind.

In spite of the wisdom of my suggestion, I'm afraid that we Americans will have a hard time stopping this unfortunate habit of always tacking our ages to our names. Even though journalists keep announcing the graying of America, ours is still a youth culture; and, like a golf tournament, we honor only low scores.

Children cannot understand how some of us have allowed our scores to get so high.

"Dad, now that you're fifty," says one of my daughters, "will we soon have to put you in a home?"

"No," I reply. "Dad is going to hang around here for a while so you can have the benefit of all his experience. You see, that's the good thing about getting older: the experience."

The problem is I keep forgetting what the experience was.

How Sick Is Satisfactory?

The one thing I wish I *could* forget is my report card from the Mayo Clinic, where I had my last annual physical. After having tested me for two days, the doctors there gave me a report card that said I was "satisfactory." Unfortunately, because the card listed no other possible grades, I have no idea where "satisfactory" stands in the Mayo marking scale. I presume it is somewhere between "Mary Lou Retton" and "comatose," but I can't be sure.

And so, my Mayo mark left me short of elated. I had been hoping for an "excellent" or at least a "rather splendid." I had been hoping some doctor would tell me, "Mr. Cosby, I'd like to put your entire physical on 'Nova' because you have the body of a nineteen-year-old." Instead, however, I seemed to have taken this physical pass-fail. Instead, I got the kind of report you get when you call a hospital to ask about a friend who has been in an accident:

"He's in stable condition."

I have never understood these particular words. Does "stable condition" mean that he's fit as a horse? Or does it mean he's not running amuck?

"Satisfactory" leaves me as dismayed as "stable" because its meaning is equally vague. Just how healthy is "satisfactory"? Does it mean that I am healthy enough to survive a heart transplant? Or a race with my son?

To be honest, I did hear more than "satisfactory" at the Mayo Clinic. In fact, I heard enough to make me resolve not to return at fifty-five because there has been a definite decline in the delightfulness of what the doctors are telling me there. The first time I went to the Mayo Clinic, at the age of forty-four, the doctor in charge of my physical said, "You have the body of a man of thirty-eight."

"Really?" I said. "Someone that old?"

"Yes, your heart is beating like Buddy Rich."

On my second visit, however, when I was forty-nine, the doctor in charge of my physical said, "You have the body of a man of forty-nine."

At least he hadn't said a *woman* of forty-nine. Nonetheless, I had aged eleven years in five, a thought that left me in despair; but then he said, "Mr. Cosby, were you an athlete?"

"Oh *yes,*" I said with a happy leap of my morale. So my varsity muscles were still there.

"That's what I thought," the doctor said, "when I saw all the scars."

"So, doctor, give it to me straight: what do you think?"

"Oh, everything is normal."

"Well, *that's* good."

"Yes, if you died tomorrow, no one would be surprised."

My Worst Runaround

I was demoralized to hear the doctor preparing for my death because I had given the Mayo Clinic the kind of effort I had always given in the Penn Relays. The problem was that the Penn Relays had no intercollegiate treadmill event, so I didn't know how to run this one at Mayo. No track coach ever taught me how to pace myself on a treadmill. Do you save your kick for the last lap? When *is* the last lap? The nurse is no track announcer.

After a few minutes on the treadmill at Mayo, I began to wonder about this last lap. My shortness of breath and my aching thighs made me realize that I was a treadmill sprinter and not a long distance man.

"I've gone . . . pretty far . . . don't you think?" I gaspingly said to the nurse.

"You're doing beautifully," she said. "You really know how to go nowhere."

"Has anyone ever . . . gone . . . this far?"

"Yes, this morning a man of seventy-eight—"

"Keep it . . . *going.*"

And so, I continued chugging along, while one of my lungs said to the other, *Don't worry, it won't be long before he faints.*

My Darling Marine

My wife has been trying for much more than a "satis-factory." A few months ago, she and a friend made a serious resolution to get into shape, a resolution that led them to a spa in the mountains of southern California that I will call Camp Happy Thighs. Outside the front gate of this palace of rejuvenation was a statue of Venus, whose classical contours were the goal of all the women who came here for a week of conditioning. Venus, of course, had no arms; but if shedding your arms was what it took to reach the proper weight, these women were ready to go for it.

To begin their stay at Camp Happy Thighs, my wife and her friend took off all their clothes and stood before mirrors for a couple of minutes so that they had a chance to develop a thorough hatred for their bodies. Every new camper at this place was required to have two basic things: cellulite and self-loathing. On her first day, the camper was supposed to stand naked in her room and say:

> Mirror, mirror, on the wall,
> Who has the flabbiest ass of all?

After working up the necessary disgust for themselves, my wife and her friend were issued their uniforms: sweatsuits, sweatsocks, and boots. And then came the first activity: not volleyball but a ten-mile march.

Now I know you may be thinking that ten miles isn't really that much, that there were women with Mao Tse-tung in '49 who marched a thousand. But remember that those women with Mao were already deep into the rice diet, while my wife and her friend had been training on capitalistic Twinkies.

Several hours later, my wife and her friend returned to their room from the march. With the little strength that she had left, my wife managed to turn on the shower; but her friend had strength enough only to make it to her bed, where she fell into a profound sleep.

Slumped on her own bed, my wife succeeded in raising the phone to her lips and ordering a meal sent to her room. In about twenty minutes, there arrived a meal for which the door did not have to be opened: the waiter could have slipped under the door the bed of lettuce with the two stalks of celery, the two slices of tomato, and the four croutons.

My wife used the next thirty seconds to eat her meal; and then, thinking that her friend would be sleeping through the night, she also ate her friend's meal, putting one crouton under her pillow to be feasted upon later.

At eleven o'clock, the friend suddenly woke up because her body was starting to eat itself: a couple of organs she was sentimental about were in danger of becoming hors d'oeuvre. Finding her dinner tray empty, the friend awakened my wife, who had decided to sleep for about a week.

"Wasn't there a dinner for me on this tray?" said the friend.

And my wife had to confess her gluttony.

"But I saved a *crouton* for you," she said.

And so, there sat the woman on her bed, trying to turn a crouton into dinner in the world's greatest land of plenty.

The next morning, my wife called me and said, "Bill, come and take me out of here."

"That isn't the spirit that built the West," I replied.

"I don't have enough spirit left to put on my

socks. I'm getting thinner and weaker by the minute."

"It worked for Gandhi."

"Bill, do you want me to *disappear?*"

"No, I kind of like seeing you around."

"Then come get me right away."

"Okay, I'll rescue you. Just wait for me; don't try to tunnel out."

Early the following day, I drove up to Camp Happy Thighs and stopped at the sentry booth outside.

"My wife has had enough chic punishment," I told the guard. "Would you please send out what's left of her?"

"Sorry," he said. "No one's allowed to come out."

"Okay, then I'll go in."

"Only if you want to start losing weight."

And so, I had to leave without seeing her. When I got home, I called her and said that she would have to serve her full sentence. There was no parole for prisoners of cellulite.

"But I miss so many *foods,*" she plaintively said, and then she described a few dozen of them.

I wanted to send her some of these foods, but I was afraid that the guards would intercept them and put her in solitary, where she would have to sit in silent salivation on a giant bed of lettuce. So I picked up a few magazines, cut out some photographs of food, and sent them to my fading beloved. I have never been able to ask her about it, but I am pretty sure that she ate them.

When she finally returned from Camp Happy Thighs, my wife continued trying to get into the condition that keeps eluding me. She began to use what I called the Canned Conscience Plan, in which Jiminy Cricket becomes a cassette: whenever the person trying to diet is tempted to have a snack, she takes a tape recorder and confesses all the food she has eaten so far that day. The theory is that hearing a review of your previous eating, especially the whipped cream that you had on your waffles at breakfast, will shame you into keeping your mouth dormant for a while.

About noon on a day not long after my wife's return from camp, I heard her voice coming from the kitchen.

"You're a liar!" she was saying. "You're a liar!"

What visitor to our house had qualified for this epithet? Our congressman? Our dentist?

And then I entered the kitchen and saw that my wife was angrily questioning the integrity of a Sony.

This is what the fear of aging does to us Americans. We sit in our kitchens and insult machines.

Does Alfalfa Leave Me in Clover?

There are inanimate things in my kitchen that *I* would like to have a few words with because I am tired of waiting for them to explain themselves to me. I am talking about all the vitamins, herbs, and health food supplements that people like me are taking as if we were eating jelly beans. The problem is that we desperate seekers of overnight health are gulping in the dark; we are swallowing drugstore dreams.

Did you ever read the label on a bottle of health food supplements? It sounds as though it is satisfying some FDA requirement for vagueness. For example, take one called Life Forever—once a day, but do you know *why?* Life Forever sounds like an afternoon soap, but its label is a story that no one can follow:

> A marine complex with special nutritional factors.

Exactly *what* is a marine complex? Camp Lejeune? And what is a marine complex with special nutritional factors? Marines who eat well?

Another elixir on my kitchen table says:

> This product is specifically formulated for those concerned with their nutritional well-being.

In other words, it is not to be taken by people who want to be sick. Moreover, it is not only rich in nebulousness, it is also "rich in omega." And what a difference *that* makes because omega is . . . well, it's either a wonderful treat for your liver or a wonderful watch.

Still another magical bottle on my kitchen table is called Acidophilus, whose label says:

> Each Acidophilus capsule provides a specially cultured strain of Lactobacilli Acidophilus and Bulgaricus, together with 100 mg. Citrus Pectin Cellulose complex. As a source of L. acidophilus in the intestinal tract to help restore and maintain a normal flora.

My feelings are mixed about this one. I don't mind taking a chance on Lactobacilli Acidophilus and Bulgaricus, even though it sounds like a Balkan disease; but do I really want my intestinal tract to have a normal flora? Do I want to turn my guts into a garden?

If You Can't Stand the Heat

No matter what all these pills do, I am counting on them to protect me from my habit of eating a succulent little hand grenade called a jalapeño pepper. A jalapeño pepper is more than just nourishment: it is also combat training because swallowing one is a test of how poised you can be with your stomach on fire.

When I was a teenager, I cockily ate jalapeño peppers in front of girls because I loved to hear them say, "Wow, this guy is *crazy!*" To be called crazy at eighteen is to receive respect; and when I felt the glow from the girls, it took my mind off the glow from the gas.

Jalapeño pepper! Jalapeño pepper! my stomach would cry when I was eighteen, and the juices would flow like fire hoses because this was a four-alarm meal. And moments after they had extinguished the pepper, the alarm sounded again:

Look out! Here comes another!

Tell him to mix it with something! Roll it in bread or asbestos!

Meanwhile, the girls kept smiling and saying, "Wow, this guy is *crazy!*"

When I am called crazy at fifty, however, I feel less respect in the word. For example, a couple of days ago, I picked up a jalapeño pepper and my wife softly said, "If you eat that thing, I will go to court and have you declared legally insane."

"Nonsense," I replied. "I used to eat these things all the time."

"Yes, and look what it's done to your brain."

She was looking at me the way a person might look at an accident in progress. I looked back at her with the confident yet idiotic smile of a man about to dive off a cliff; and then I put the pepper in my mouth and began to chew.

This time, my stomach sent up no cry of panic. This time, the fire department simply went on strike; and, like Atlanta, I burned through the night.

4

DO THE LEGS GO BEFORE THE MIND?

My Son, the Blur

One of the great mistakes that can be made by a man
of my age is to get involved in athletic competition
with children—unless, of course, they are under six.
And even then, stay away from hide-and-seek.

In spite of my awareness of this athletic truth, a
few years ago I could not resist luring my son Ennis
out to the track because I wanted to see how my
genes looked in a newer model of me; and I was also
intoxicated by a dream of sitting in the stands at the
1988 Olympics and proudly watching my only son.
Of course, if I do see Ennis at the 1988 Olympics, he
will be in the seat beside me because he lacks my
competitive zeal. If you are trying to make the
Olympic track team, it is a definite disadvantage if
you hate to run.

Even though my music is the theme from *Chariots of Fire* and Ennis's theme is "Bidin' My Time," I began taking him out to tracks with me when he was fourteen and I was forty-six. Wherever I am working, whether I'm taping my television show in Brooklyn or doing a film in Los Angeles or playing a nightclub in Las Vegas, I always spend some time exercising at a nearby track. In every workout, I try to run at least two or three miles and also a couple of quarters. The quarter mile has always been my event: I ran it in college; and now, in my days of falling apart, I am running it in masters track meets, where my fastest time at the age of forty-six was fifty-eight seconds.

Although he is tall and thin, Ennis prefers lacrosse to track, possibly because lacrosse players don't throw up as often as track men. A smart young man, he learned early that there is loneliness and pain in running, no matter how mystical the trendy joggers make it sound. Americans have become so solemnly pious about running that every CPA in a sweatsuit expects to see God after dragging his flab down the road for a couple of miles. But long before he sees God, he is liable to see his lunch.

At the time that I first talked Ennis into working out with me, I ran a two-hundred-yard dash against him and always won. At my age, you have to take your sporting triumphs where you find them, even if you find them in races with boys who don't want to run.

When he turned fifteen, Ennis was six feet tall and loose and springy and still did not want to run. He kept giving me excuses, which I heard with all the sensitivity of Fred Flintstone. You know all that sensitivity of mine that you read about in *Fatherhood*? Well, I don't take it to the track.

Trying to whip up Ennis's enthusiasm for track was like trying to whip up a fly's enthusiasm for taking a tour of a spider's web. Whenever he came for a workout, he came late, but I did not mind. Had he come earlier, I would have had to listen to more muttering.

But the maddening thing was that the boy was a natural athlete; and so, I kept trying hard to encourage him.

"Ennis, you can *do* it," I told him one day.

"Of *course* I can," he replied. "But I don't *want* to."

At last, I was able to talk him into running a quarter mile, and my feelings about the result were decidedly mixed: he did the quarter in fifty-nine seconds, a time that made me proud; but it was a time that I could have beaten only by going flat out, and flat out is a condition in which I am not a happy man.

However, I decided that I *would* have a race with him in the two-hundred-yard dash. And so, we took off and I quickly moved out ahead of him. After about the first hundred yards, he seemed discouraged because I was running so well, and I even wondered if he might be thinking of conceding the race to me. In spite of his having the incalculable advantage of being fifteen against my forty-seven, he was competing halfheartedly. I have always wanted my contemporaries to compete this way, but I didn't like the style in my son.

I finally won the race in the time of twenty-seven seconds, two seconds slower than if I had gone flat out. I had been so busy thinking about my time and my pride that I never received the message my poor son had been trying to send:

Dad, how about something else—*like crazy eights?*

But I would not give up.

Cosby and Custer.

The following year, when Ennis was sixteen and I was forty-eight, I dragged him out to a track that was made of cement, just like my head. By this point, Ennis had stopped muttering: he had simply tuned out the pathetic exhortations of the aging jock who was trying to recycle his varsity genes. I still was trying to talk him into running a quarter mile with me, but Ennis seemed more inclined to taking a shot at a twenty-five-yard dash.

"Okay," I told him one day, "here's what we're going to do now: we're going to run seven-eighths speed; nice and relaxed."

"How far?" he replied.

"Oh . . . straight ahead a ways."

"But how *far?*"

"I'm afraid I can't say."

I couldn't say because I needed *some* concession to my age. By not announcing the distance of the race, I was making it possible for myself to stop any time I wanted. I was also making it *impossible* for Ennis to pace himself. I am nothing if not a sportsman.

And so, we both took off. At the beginning of the race, I was running at seven-eighths of my speed, but Ennis was just taking it easy because his goal was not the finish line but the avoidance of pain. My legs were churning, for I knew that if Ennis decided to open up, he would leave me like a train pulling out of a station. Even while he ran at three-quarters speed, his power was depressingly clear: his three-quarters moved considerably better than my seven-eighths.

That was the day that Bill Cosby invented a new track and field event: the hundred-and-three-yard dash. It's a middle distance race for me.

As Satchel Said, Don't Look Back

One day while I was running on the UCLA track, pretending that I was on my way to winning still another decathlon, I saw a boy from the college track team who was running too—and suddenly I stopped, transfixed by the sight of someone moving with a blend of grace, speed, and power so splendid that I could only sigh and think:

There goes nineteen.

I soon discovered that this young man's time for three hundred yards was thirty-three seconds. Mine was forty. Thirty-three was close to the world's record and I could not dream of doing that, even in my most demented moments, which were coming quite frequently these days.

But what would I have to do to get my time down to thirty-seven or thirty-eight? I asked myself.

Get a leg transplant, I answered. *For a start.*

At my age, the hardest thing to do is accept what you *are* and not torture yourself with visions of what you used to be. What you are is a jackass if you think you can come even close to catching up to your old self, for there is no race more ridiculous than one in which you are running against a ghost.

In spite of my awareness of this melancholy truth, I cannot stop carrying a mental picture of myself from my early years, a picture that still seems current when I run two or even three steps. In those first steps, I am always nineteen; but I age fast around the first turn, never understanding why. I haven't *seen* the rust forming on me.

Fly the Unfriendly Skies

Not only can I never catch my old self as a runner, but in trying to catch my old self as a high jumper, I enter an area of poignant ludicrousness, and ludicrous poignancy too.

My first visit to this area was the first time that I decided to high jump in a masters track meet. The best jump I had ever made at Temple was six feet seven; I had just missed at six feet nine. However, in the masters meet, the bar was set for me at five feet. I cleared it but felt no elation because five feet is *nothing*. People convalescing from surgery can clear five feet.

For the next round, the officials raised the bar to five feet three. I walked up to it, studied it, and suddenly realized something was wrong. When I had cleared six-seven, I had been looking *up* at the bar, but I was now looking *down*. It was like one of the tricks that my trifocals played on me.

No matter what the problem was, as I made my first approach to the bar, I was possessed by another of those moments of derangement in which I felt that I was the same person I had always been. And this same person hit the bar and knocked it off, a truly rotten jump for a man of twenty-three.

It was absurd that I couldn't clear something I once had been able to *hop* over after taking only two steps—and while wearing a *warm-up* suit. I concluded that there simply must have been something wrong with my timing. And I was right: I was born in 1937.

I still had two more chances to clear this height of five feet three and my confidence remained unshaken. I kept telling myself that I was a man who once had cleared six-seven. I kept telling myself that I was a man who still could clear six feet. And, pathetically, I was *listening* to me.

When they called my name for my second try, I clenched my teeth, filled my lungs, ran up to the bar, and hit it again. As I looked at the bar on the ground, I began to laugh incredulously. Other competitors were laughing too, but incredulous they surely were not. They believed that Cosby had missed again.

"I don't know what's wrong with this equipment," I told one of them. "You see, my height is six-seven."

"Of course it is," he said in a tone that is popular in nursery schools.

"This height is for my *wife*."

"Of course it is."

"No, no," I said, "you don't understand."

But he *did* understand. Those masters always understand the newest man to be pitied.

At this point, I was more than just embarrassed: I was deeply angry at myself. Sitting there in the infield of the track and starting to wonder what decade it was, I finally came to a moment of truth and realized what was wrong: the flaw in my jumping—besides, of course, always running into the bar—was my form. Therefore, on my next turn, I would abandon my classical grace and I would "Bogart" the jump, a word that meant I would muscle myself over it with the sheer grit of Humphrey Bogart.

And so, Bill Bogey now was ready for his third and final try, fiercely determined that a blend of will power, muscle power, and Warner Brothers movies would take him over the bar. My plan was inspired: I would make my run to the bar, hit my mark precisely, and then Bogart my way toward the sky.

Once more, they called my name. Once more, the other masters smiled. And once more, I made my run, a seven-step approach. Then I planted my foot, sprang up with all the power at my command, and hit the bar again.

A masters track meet can be a richly educational experience. At this one, I learned that a man of my age should never try a Bogart. A George Burns is what he ends up with.

My Joints Are Jumpin'

The problem is not simply that we foolishly keep getting older. The problem is that, in spite of the American craze for fitness, in spite of health clubs and aerobics and Jane Fonda's thighs, we are not the jocks we used to be because we no longer plunge into sports with the total, flat-out, slightly insane zeal we once had. We may be jogging nicely by ourselves, but we no longer play team sports as hard or as well. There is more coordination in our outfits than our jump shots.

A good example of this vanished zeal is my own early conditioning in the Asphalt Athletic Club: the streets of north Philadelphia. When I was a teenage boy in a housing project there, I lived sports the way few teenagers do today. On a typical summer morning, I got up, washed my face, and skipped a hearty breakfast; and then I went out to meet my friends. I was clean and empty; but I was also full of a lust for all-day competition that has disappeared from a land where so many kids spend so many days at malls, letting their minds and bodies turn to custard in video arcades.

When I say all-day, I *mean* all-day: the boys and I played baseball, basketball, football, and stickball for eight or nine hours with no breaks. From time to time, one of our mothers would come down to the Asphalt A.C. and try to drag one of the members home for some forced feeding.

"You've got to *eat!*" this strange woman would say.

"Why?" her son would reply with a logic all his own.

"Just take my word for it: every day or two, you've got to eat."

"But I'll miss the *second half.*"

"You'll end up in the *hospital.*"

"Do they have a team there?"

This boy afraid of missing the second half had already played eighteen second halves, but now he was getting ready to peak. Today's teenagers, however, are a different breed. They play half court games instead of full court ones; and after a while, one of them will say, "Hey, I'm beat. Let's go rent some videos."

In my old neighborhood, a boy stopped playing

when he began to lose his pulse. And then he became the referee.

On summer nights, we often played until it got dark—and then we played more. There is no challenge greater in the whole world of sport than coming to bat in a night game on a field that has no lights. The pitcher doesn't need much to handle you, just a general idea of where his catcher is. On that field of asphalt-turf, there *were* a few streetlights, but they were good only for illuminating the top halves of fly balls. To handle a grounder, you needed the headlights of an oncoming Chevrolet.

Because of the intensity and duration of such competition, I was in wonderful shape to play organized sport in high school and college. This wonderful shape did not keep me from dropping the baton in a big relay at Penn, but I dropped it with a very muscular arm. In the years since then, I have come to realize that if a person sustained some of this intensity after his college days, he would be in better shape in his forties and fifties. Some of the masters I've known have trained that way and it shows in their running, and also in the hearty way they laugh at me.

If a man in his middle years does not sustain his conditioning with a certain intensity, he will not be able to counteract the effects of time; and, after an injury, he will not be able to heal the way he once did. In fact, life for him will seem to become one long quiet injury: he will begin to hear sounds in his body that belong in a car that is being recalled.

What's that clicking? he will ask himself. *I'm supposed to* jell, *not* click. *And what's that ticking? If you're clicking, you shouldn't tick too. I need a grease and lube job. I wonder if a little silicone on my elbows and knees would help.*

This man has reached an age when he has to be careful about where he sits. I am not talking about checking a chair to see if it's holding a plate of hors d'oeuvre: I am talking about the mistake of sitting in a chair so soft that he cannot get back up without making a noise. If the most sublime ascent a man can make is up Mount Everest, the least sublime is rising out of a chair with grunts. Moreover, there is nothing more demoralizing than coming into the living room and having one of your daughters say, "Here, Dad, you take the piano bench."

Franklin D. Who?

During much of the time that I am sitting, no matter what the state of the chair, I speak a language that is foreign to people under thirty because from time to time I refer to things that happened more than three years ago. No part of aging is more dismaying than losing your references, than getting a blank look from a young person to whom you have just mentioned the name of someone obscure, like Paul McCartney.

"Paul McCartney? . . . Paul McCartney?" this young person is liable to say. "Wait a minute—I *think* I've heard of him. Didn't he used to be with a group called Wings or Wangs?"

George Santayana once said, "Those who cannot remember the past are condemned to repeat it." But the problem is: Who was George Santayana? Stop fifty people under forty—or forty people under fifty —and they will tell you that Santayana was either a shortstop for the Indians, the president of Guatemala, or the man who attacked the Alamo. The Alamo, of course, was an Italian battleship.

Two or three entire generations of Americans know Joe DiMaggio as the man who sold Mr. Coffee. In talking to these generations, if you happen to make a slip and refer to something medieval like Fats Waller or Franklin D. Roosevelt, you brand yourself a living fossil. Like an agent in the OSS, you must bear in mind that just one little slip can give you away. And *that* was a little slip by *me:* the Office of Strategic Services was an organization from World War II, and World War II is a dangerous reference if you are trying to make contact with the underage enemy, with the people who think Pearl Harbor is a new rock star.

Other slips that can reveal you as a relic are saying "oaktag" instead of "poster board," "phonograph" instead of "stereo," and "French Equatorial Africa" instead of "Chad." Moreover, *never* let the younger people know that you think a compact disc is a sturdy spine; and *never* say to them, "That was before your time," because the last full moon was before their time.

A few weeks ago, I happened to say to a member of this Born Yesterday crowd, "I'm glad Miles Davis is feeling well."

I had made another slip, of course, for my young listener didn't know Miles Davis from Jefferson Davis. One of his *friends,* however, knew Jefferson Davis: that great lead guitarist with the Jefferson Airplane.

In addition to never mentioning something that happened more than three weeks ago, there is one other thing you must never say:

"When I was your age."

You were *never* their age. You were older in the womb.

5

TIME LURCHES ON

The Blackest Gray

When I reached my mid-forties, I began to get some gray hair, but it did not upset me. I didn't run to the drugstore for a bottle of Grecian Formula to turn back the clock because I knew that my gray simply meant I had entered a new phase of manhood, the phase of debonairly falling apart. In fact, not only did the gray not upset me, but I even liked the touches of it on my temples and the little streak of it in my beard. It added twenty points to my IQ.

But then one morning, the march of time suddenly trampled me: I found a gray hair in my pubic zone, where I had always liked to wear my hair black, and I felt depressed, for gray did not seem to add any distinction to my crotch. It was a thoroughly undistinguished sign of age. I had come full circle: from the time that I yearned to see my first pubic hair to the time that I saw the first pubic hair I didn't want.

How well I remember the thrill of getting that first pubic hair when I was a boy! It is not the kind of boyhood memory that Norman Rockwell celebrated, but it was nevertheless a precious mammalian milestone to me. Before that first pubic hair arrived, I had been embarrassed whenever other boys saw me in the nude at the pool where we swam.

It's coming! I wanted to tell them. *It's definitely on the way!*

But in despair I kept wondering, *How long will it take? Could I* please *have an estimated time of arrival? Will it be happening in my lifetime?*

I was already thirteen and all my friends of thirteen *had* their pubic hair nicely in place; they were already men, while *I* belonged to a different and really stupid generation. Whenever these hairy show-offs came to the pool, they removed their underpants with a flourish and seemed to take forever in putting on their trunks. I, however, *arrived* in my trunks and kept them on even in the shower so my baldness could not be seen and reported to the Philadelphia *Bulletin*.

In those distressing days, my head was constantly bowed, not in prayer but pubic inspection, for I was rooting for my roots. My doubts were much darker than anything growing in my groin.

And then, one fine morning, puberty smiled on me. I looked down for my daily inspection and discovered that my pelvis had bloomed: a single hair had appeared. My manhood was certified and my spirit soared.

Been waiting, eh? the hair seemed to say.

Do you happen to know if any of your friends are coming? I asked him. *There's room for plenty more.*

They're on their way, he replied.

When?

Take a good look down there.

I quickly looked and saw faint hints of happy arrivals: a fine peach fuzz in the proper area. And then I discovered that this fuzz got dark whenever I wet it, so I dramatically increased my number of showers.

"Bill is such a *clean* boy," I heard my mother saying to a friend one afternoon.

"And cleanliness is next to godliness," the friend replied.

Both women were blessedly unaware that this

particular cleanliness was as far from godliness as my gonads could be.

About a week later, a second hair appeared, equally lovely and intoxicating, and then a third and a fourth. I was terribly proud, for it didn't take much to make me proud in those days.

Soon, however, the hairs started moving down the inside of my thighs.

Okay, that's enough, I told them. *You can stop now.*

But my hormones were on a roll and the hair continued to come: in fact, it was curling up my behind.

Stop it! I said, feeling like a budding werewolf.

I was about to dive into a vat of depilatory when the growth finally stopped; and there, crowning it all, sat the pubic hair, rich and dark—until the awful day thirty-seven years later when I saw the first gray one. The pubic hair that had come to me as a boy was a sign of manhood, but what was the message of this first *gray* one? I knew it well, a two-part message for a man turning fifty:

My body no longer produced lean meat. And I should start to shower in the dark.

As more of this lower gray appears, I have been wondering: would I be too vain if I started using

Grecian Formula in a place that only my wife and doctor ever see? My wife, of course, might not learn about it for a while because she sees the total me less than ever these days. Just as I no longer can go one-on-one in basketball the way I once did, I also lack the stamina to go one-on-one in bed the way I did in my salad days. In spite of the profound love I have for my wife, sex at my age has become exhausting, which leaves me yearning for a younger body, or longing for a good nap. A man of my age comes home late from the office, has dinner, takes a shower, ignores a few bills, and finally makes it into bed. Discovering another person in that bed, and dimly aware that this person is a different sex, he starts to make his move.

"Not tonight," says his wife.

And the man rolls over with a smile.

Thank you very much, he silently says.

His heart had not been in the mood, nor any other part. All he had really wanted to do was to go on record.

My wife probably feels that our bed has become a G movie, but I am actually in tune with the times, for recent surveys have revealed that most women would rather cuddle than have sex, and I am the Clark Gable of cuddlers. I don't need Dr. Ruth because I am tuned to Dr. Seuss.

Wasted on the Young

At least my wife and her cuddler are growing older together: we're in sync because neither of us has dived into one of the many fountains of youth that are bubbling all over this age-fearing land. We haven't panicked about getting older and started trying to look like our children. Last year, Americans spent more than one billion dollars on lotions, potions, and surgery so that they could be confused with their children instead of just being confused *by* them.

A few days ago on television, I saw a commercial for a liquid detergent. Two different women were displaying their hands side by side for the nation to admire.

"Can you tell the mother's hands from her daughter's?" an announcer asked me.

"Of course," I replied. "The daughter's hands are the ones that have just been in her mother's wallet."

What is the *point* of all this? That mothers should be impersonating their daughters? That all of us should be one big happy teenage generation? Can you imagine a more frightening horror film than one in which all the adults in America turned into teenagers?

This is a wonderful country, but the people in it are quite insane about reversing the aging process. They are trying to wake up every morning heading for yesterday. Where will it all end? Since there seems to be a stampede back to the womb, it will all end with one fetus trying to call out to another, "I'm less developed than *you!*"

I know one woman who puts bee pollen on her skin to keep it looking young. She is now a woman who could fertilize a flower with a sneeze, but she is driven to turn back the clock to Teenage Saving Time. Other women are putting potato peelings and tea bags on their eyelids; some are covering their faces with Italian mud; and a newspaper recently told of a woman who put cement on her face as a cosmetic mask and couldn't remove it.

One of these days, I will walk into somebody's home and ask, "What's that new statue in your living room, Newt?"

"'That's no statue," he will say, "that's Mother. Lovely skin, don't you think?"

"Absolutely. Not a pothole in sight."

For twenty years, I have known one particular woman, who now does not look anything like the woman I met twenty years ago *or* the woman I knew *three months* ago. She has had plastic surgery so often that her features have changed and she is now wearing someone else's face; the essence of her has disappeared. She is very happy because she doesn't look old. She does, however, look mismatched. She is a new kind of female impersonator.

Plastic surgery has been creating hundreds of thousands of people like this, people whose parts don't match, people who seem to have been assembled by astigmatic elves. If you put a boyish face on a man of seventy-three who can't bend over, you have a new kind of centaur—and the horse's ass is the man who had the surgery.

Which Teenager Is
in Charge Here?

I must admit, of course, that I am more conscious of youth than I should be, especially now that the people in charge are suddenly looking so young, people like doctors and congressmen and cops. How can you accept a speeding ticket from someone who looks as though he is dressed up for the school play? And how can you have your blood pressure taken by someone who looks as though he should be asking you if he can borrow the car?

The television business is the worst one for a fossil like me because it is run by people who look as though they are planning the senior prom. The problem that we ancients have with such post-teen executives is the one I have mentioned: they don't know certain references, like World War II.

"Oh yes, of course," said one TV executive to a writer I know who had mentioned World War II. "That was the one with Japan, wasn't it?"

Fortunately, my hearing is going, so I don't always have to hear the children in charge saying things like this.

"Well, you're around that age," the ear doctor says. "There's a little loss, but nothing we didn't expect."

"Well, you're around that age," the periodontist says. "There's a little bone loss, but nothing we didn't expect."

"Well, you're around that age," the ophthalmologist says. "There's a little loss in seeing walls, but nothing we didn't expect."

"Well, you're around that age," the psychiatrist says. "There's a little more stupidity, but nothing we didn't expect."

What I pray is that all the parts of me do not shut down all at once. What the man of fifty has to avoid is an orchestrated falling-apart.

Just as the people in authority start to look too young to you at this age, your friends from the past start to look too old, especially if you haven't seen them for thirty or forty years. One of Cosby's rules for keeping happy at fifty is to never see someone whom you haven't seen for more than ten years because that person will have gone from looking thirty to looking sixty-three.

For this reason, I avoid attending reunions of my college class because the people I'd meet at them would suddenly look like their own fathers and I would be searching for the kid who was lost inside.

"Hi, there," someone vaguely familiar would say to me. "I'm Sam Cooke, '58."

And you would smile at him and think: *Sam, you don't look that young.*

"Hi, Sam," you would say. "I'm Danny Marks, '58."

And *he* would think: *That must be his pulse.*

The conversation might be pleasant enough until he said, "Danny, do you happen to have the time?"

And now you are in trouble because he sees you are wearing a watch, but he doesn't know that you can't read it in the dim light of this room, especially because you have left off your glasses in a heartbreaking effort to look less than sixty-three. You have a pretty good idea it is early evening, but the precise positions of the minute and hour hands are just rumors to you. For the last few months, your watch has been a bracelet that says Bulova.

Slip Off Some Skin

A class reunion is the setting for one particular radio commercial about getting older that I keep hearing. In this commercial, a woman fools everyone at her reunion because she has used a miraculous skin cream to remove all signs of age.

"Eleanor Feeney!" cries one of her classmates. "Is that really *you?* I can't *believe* it! You haven't aged a day in twenty-five years!"

"Aging is for suckers," Eleanor replies. "The only *real* Americans are young ones."

"What's your *secret?* Have you gone to Switzerland to get those new injections of ground goat placenta?"

"No, I just stay in Pittsburgh and erase my face with Skin Me."

"Skin Me? What's *that?* A new kind of sandpaper?"

"No, it's a magical rejuvenating cream that manages to combine feminine softness with a sulfuric acid base."

"Well, Eleanor, your face looks *incredible.*"

"So far I've knocked off nineteen years."

"Have you ever thought of finishing the job and rubbing out that nose?"

"No, I just erase enough so that people will think I'm my own daughter."

Listening to this commercial, I think of my own wife, who doesn't need Skin Me or Easy Off or Vanish. She naturally looks so young that some people who've seen us together have actually taken her for my daughter. Of course, I have days when Pearl Bailey could be taken for my daughter too.

And Maybe I Can Also Walk on Water

Being fifty has an unreality for me. For example, on a television commercial, I hear my friend Ed McMahon talking about life insurance that older people can get and I think, *It's nice that older people can get life insurance.* But suddenly I realize that Ed is talking about *me.* His benevolent company will take a fling and insure a declining body like mine, probably laying off the risk with Lloyd's of London.

Am I really that old? Am I really that close to falling down, breaking my hip, and checking out? What a shock it was to be struck by this thought! No matter how many years have passed since I was a boy, I am *still* that boy and I will never be able to see myself as being old enough to break my hip in a fall, unless a linebacker landed on top of me. Breaking a hip in Ed McMahon's world leads to dying and dying certainly has never been a part of my plans, not for Kryptonite Cosby. At fifty, I know the way of all flesh intellectually, but a part of me still feels as immortal as a child. Every authentic child, of course, believes he is immortal and sees all older people as being part of God's hit list.

I remember myself at the age of thirteen, when I had such a list: all the people I loved who were supposed to die. As the oldest, my grandparents came first, to be followed by some aunts and uncles who were in shaky shape. (One of these uncles, Jack, was a diabetic, and every time he ate a cookie, I took out my black suit.) And after the aunts and uncles came my parents, but I hoped that they would stay on the active part of the list for another eighty or ninety years, avoiding all the diseases that kept such a list in a state of flux.

The last name on this hit parade was mine, but it was strictly an honorary entry—honorary, that is, when I first put it down. But as I grew older and the people ahead of me began to disappear, the reality of death became a little clearer to me, although it still was something that happened only to those people who had tossed me up in the air when I was small, those people who had been foolish enough to allow themselves to turn forty. Little did I dream in those days that a man of sixty could actually have sex and not be an act in the circus.

I remember one day at the age of fifteen, when I heard my mother and father talking about a friend of theirs named Henry, who had just died at forty-three. They were shocked by his death, but I was not. At fifteen, I felt that Henry *should* have shuffled off: forty-three was the proper time to drop dead. Needless to say, at fifteen, an age when the brain of the male is still in a semi-primitive state, no boy is aware that Arnold Palmer, Satchel Paige, Gordie Howe, Al Oerter, Josh Gibson, and George Blanda all have been brilliant athletes at precisely forty-three, the age at which John F. Kennedy became the youngest man ever elected President of the United States.

However, when *I* reached forty-three, I changed my mind about Henry's death and decided that he had gone shockingly young. I also decided that if I still wanted to be immortal, I would need help, either from a divinity or a drugstore. Today, at fifty, I am looking with more interest than ever at the medical researchers, cheering them on to cure everything from hypertension to hives. The average person wonders every day about the weather, but I never think about that. I think instead about when Macy's will be getting artificial hearts.

Immortality is a long shot, I admit; but *somebody* has to be first.

Lend Me Your Ears

There is a saying that goes:

Youth is a gift of nature;
Age is a work of art.

Well, I hate to disagree with Confucius or Hallmark, but if age is a work of art, the artist is one who belongs in the subway and not in the Louvre. I have heard about people aging gracefully and I'm sure that there must have been five or ten; but most of us merely clump along toward the golden years—and find when we arrive that the gold standard has been dropped. Therefore, as I have grown older, I have studied people as they approached these tarnished years so that at least I could avoid unfortunate patterns of behavior and break down with originality.

As one example of my geriatric scholarship, I have studied the way people with hearing problems pretend that such problems do not exist. I admit that most of what *I* hear, especially from children and members of the federal government, is not worth hearing; but, nevertheless, I do feel obliged to process the sound. However, many people with poor hearing refuse to wear a hearing aid and instead prefer to take a guess at what you have said. When you have finished a conversation with one of these people, you say, "Okay, we'll talk on the phone."

And he replies, "Yes, we'll take out a loan."

Not all these people have worked with pneumatic drills or rock bands: many have simply lost some of their hearing in the process of getting older and life for them has become a silent film. I feel sympathy for them, of course. Just as I have lost a few steps on the track (yes, seventeen can still be called a few), they have lost a few decibels; but I do wish they would stop getting angry whenever I point out that they have guessed the wrong titles for their silent film.

"Mr. Twinkle called you," one such person will say.

"Mr. *Twinkle?*" you reply. "I don't *know* any Mr. Twinkle."

"Well, he called anyway."

"It must have been Mr. *Finkel,* not Twinkle."

"Well, that's what he *said,*" this person will tell you with an edge in his voice. *"Twinkle.* Maybe he changed it because he wants to be a star."

"Did he leave a number?" you ask him, having given up your search for the name.

"Yes," he says, "here it is. Zero-one-one eight-four-one-five."

"Zero-one-one eight-four-one-*five?* That's Southern *Japan.* That's *Kyushu.*"

"Gesundheit."

For some reason, people who have lost a part of their hearing are even more vain than people who need glasses: they often refuse to wear hearing aids. And when they do wear them, they often feel too proud to turn them on. Once again, I am sympathetic: a hearing aid that is on sometimes makes a high piercing sound, as if it is calling all cocker spaniels, a sound that can be caused by the contact made when the person with the hearing aid gets involved in a cuddle.

"I want you, Eleanor," a man might say to a woman with a hearing aid. He makes a move to embrace her and then her security system goes off, telling him not to nibble her ear. Perhaps if hearing aids were made so that they did not sound alarms, more people would turn them on and I would get fewer messages to call Mr. Tinkle, Mr. Bumble, or Mr. Paul Revere.

Do Not Go Bananas into That Good Night

The reason we must be tolerant with older people who have lost some of their hearing or vision or mind is simply that *we* will almost certainly have such loss if we enjoy the good fortune to live long enough to fall apart. In fact, life plays a great joke on middle-aged people: it teaches them how foolish they were when they swore years ago that they would never become as crazy as their parents. A study of your mother and father is a worthwhile thing to do because it gives you a nice little preview of your own late-blooming looniness.

For example, a friend of mine who just turned fifty was recently entering a theater with his mother of seventy-two.

"Tom," said his mother sweetly, "maybe you should go to the bathroom before the show starts."

Tom must be prepared for his own arrival at seventy-two, when he will say to his son of forty-eight as they walk into a hockey game, "Ernie, are you still remembering to brush your teeth up and down?"

Unfortunately, the man of fifty needs all the coaching he can get, especially when his bladder is full, for it now takes him longer to urinate—sometimes the better part of an inning. I step up to a urinal full of dreams of instant relief, only to find my body saying, *Why are we here?*

And I reply, *Because we can't do this in the living room or the car. Send a message to the bladder to get in gear.*

A few seconds later, while I continue to stand there like some earthy Roman statue, my body reports, *The bladder says he's asleep. He says to just settle for washing your hands.*

One of the most embarrassing moments for a man of fifty is to have to urinate under pressure with a line behind him, a problem that arises in a theater, a ballpark, and the Washington Monument. I always feel that the man right behind me can *tell* if I am faking it, if I am being the Marcel Marceau of the john.

It is one thing to fail to perform with a woman: she can give you a kiss and say you are still wonderful and it doesn't matter. But when you fail to perform at a urinal, it *does* matter: you leave in worse shape than when you arrived, and there is never any comfort from the man behind.

A Penny Saved Is Worthless Too

JESUS SAVES is a sign that all of us have seen. But Jesus was a man who *didn't* save, who didn't amass a great mound of meaningless memorabilia, because he never had a closet and he died at thirty-three. By thirty-three, I already had been saving my program from the 1958 Penn-Temple football game for nine years; and I *still* have this program in a drawer of my desk, the drawer where I file my old wine corks. If there is ever a bull market in 1958 football programs, I am ready to make a killing. Of course, I probably would not sell it because it means too much to me. At least, I *think* it does; I can't really remember.

I have not saved certain documents from last year that the Internal Revenue Service would love to see, but I've saved that semi-precious program; and I also have a story from the New York *Times* of July 17, 1976, on the effect of rainfall on the coffees of Costa Rica, a *Farmer's Almanac* for 1963 inscribed by my CPA, a thought-provoking brochure about the future of People Express, a map of Akron, Ohio (including Cuyahoga Falls), and a booklet called "The Story of Zinc." Why have I saved these things? Because there's a loose wire in my head? Yes, partly that; but also because I am growing older, and the older you get, the harder it is to throw things out. In fact, one of the first principles of the universe (Newton missed it, but Cosby didn't) is:

The more worthless the thing, the more you treasure it.

Of course, the 1976 newspaper story on Costa

Rican sogginess, the inscribed *Farmer's Almanac* of 1963, the People Express brochure, the map of Akron, and "The Story of Zinc" all happen to be of inherent value; but I also have other things, like the menus of nine Chinese restaurants and two New Jersey license plates, whose value might be questionable.

And so, such clutter keeps piling up in your closets and corners and drawers, while you keep wondering if your old Pennsylvania Railroad timetables are of more sentimental or monetary value. Will they one day take their place beside early Superman comics? Early Captain Marvels are a cornerstone of my brother's portfolio.

In spite of either kind of value that may have been attained by your junk, there still are moments when the junk suddenly overwhelms you and you say with a gratifying urgency:

Someday I've got to clean this stuff out.

It is a wonderful feeling to make a firm resolution for the indefinite future.

If you ever do get around to actually cleaning out the junk, you find yourself involved in a bittersweet business because the junk is the memories of your life, even if you can't remember half of it. (Does a man who is drowning see his whole closet pass by?)

You look at a piece of paper, an advertisement for a laundry, and you wonder why you have saved it. Are you emotionally involved with starch?

You have saved this for a reason, your memory says.

What reason? you ask.

Damned if I can remember, your memory replies.

Then let's throw it out.

But it feels *important. Better save it and throw out these canceled checks instead.*

In a drawer near the laundry ad, you find a plastic grizzly bear with a thermometer in its stomach, a souvenir of Yellowstone Park. This souvenir was worthless when you bought it and its value will probably decrease. It is so worthless, in fact, that its thermometer says the temperature in your desk is forty-three. It has no valid connection to either climate or you; and you have already forgotten the difference between Yellowstone and Asbury Park. Nevertheless, something will always keep you from throwing it away, some nutty notion that you would miss it. You feel that there will come a night when your wife will turn to you and say, "Honey, let's put on some music and play with the plastic bear."

Even more precious than the ad for the laundry

or the plastic bear or "The Story of Zinc" is every single thing your children have ever brought home from school, including the letter about lice.

"I *have* to save these eight hundred and fifty finger paintings," I once told a friend, who was wondering why there was no room in my garage for my car. "Not just for sentimental value, but also because my four daughters happen to be geniuses. No one has smeared like that since the Renaissance."

"Well, *my* daughter was toilet trained before she was two," the friend proudly said.

"Too bad it's nothing you can save," I said. "By the way, would you like to come down to the basement and see my youngest daughter's crayon work? It will remind you of Van Gogh."

"Van Gogh never worked with crayons."

"Because he wasn't good enough."

As we get older, we even save articles of clothing that we will never wear again because we already have nine or twenty-six of the same thing. For example, one of my daughters recently gave me a new tie. However, like many American men, I am wearing ties less often than ever before, so I added my daughter's to an inactive rack that included rep ties from the fifties, paisley ties from the sixties, wide ties from the seventies, pencil-thin ties from the eighties, and one tie that looked like a timeless barber pole. In fact, I have so many of them that if I tied them all end-to-end, I could be the equipment man for a prison break; but *still* I cannot throw one out.

Another nice example of muddled conservation is that I also cannot throw out a single name from my telephone book, even when the person has passed to that great area code in the sky. And so, my phone book is a living memorial to 1964, full of the dead, the divorced, and the departed for Venezuela.

The telephone book of a middle-aged man is like Walt Disney's view of America: everyone forever living happily together. My telephone book has dozens of people that I probably never will call again, especially the dead ones; and yet something deep inside me—deep stupidity, I suspect—prevents me from removing their names.

"This is not a phone book, it's a shrine," my wife said last week while looking through the alphabetized story of my life. "The only name you don't have in here is Booker T. Washington."

"I'd better take care of that," I said. "I think I owe him a call."

Applause for My Keys

The saving of the names in your telephone book, like the saving of the finger paintings and the booklets and the bear, is simply a refusal to let go of the past, an attempt to keep alive your sweet yesterdays. Most of us want to save yesterday because we think it was better than today, because memory has a sugarcoater and we can never remember pain. (If *women* could remember pain, we would be a nation of single-child families.) What we have to keep telling ourselves is that *these* are the good old days, even though I sometimes need the Roto-Rooter man to clear my throat, even though the executive in charge of my act at Radio City Music Hall sounds to me on the phone like someone who should be taking out my daughter, and even though my wife just gave me a key ring that whistles when I clap so I can find it.

We have to be mellow about the signs of turning fifty in these good old days, signs like this key ring. Because I was given the ring just a couple of days ago,

I haven't had to use it yet; and the first time I do, it will be my luck to leave my keys beyond the range of the clap and call a Doberman pinscher instead. Of course, it doesn't really matter if I leave the keys beyond the range of even a howitzer because I can't remember where the car is parked anyway.

Polly, Are You Crackers?

Whether or not these truly are the good old days, I cannot deny that I am getting older in a country where a major religion is the Church of Acne. The median age of our people has now risen to thirty-one and we talk an excellent game of appreciating older people. Nevertheless, age discrimination is still a popular pastime in America, where the seven ages of man have become preschooler, Pepsi generation, baby boomer, mid-lifer, empty-nester, senior citizen, and organ donor.

On the air and in the press, the message keeps coming at me: Erase my lines and color my hair and use the Anti-Aging Diet to chew my way to yesterday. And the message never stops: Get *younger,* get *younger!* Tote that cream and lift that face! I am going in the wrong *direction* by waking up each morning one day older.

In spite of the Gospel According to Callowness, I do try so hard to convince myself that these are the good old days, and so do people like Polly Bergen, who said two years ago, "Fifty-three is what I am and I can't find another age that I like better." But I cannot help wondering how hard she looked. Did she try twenty-seven? And what about nine? When *I* was nine, I was clapping not for key rings but the rings of a circus. I was clapping for a clown who was teaching an old dog how to play dead. Now *I'm* an old dog and people say I cannot learn new tricks; but this of course isn't true: you *can* teach an old dog new tricks. You just don't want to see the dog doing them.

6

FIFTY IS NIFTY AFTER ALL

The Looniness of the Long Distance Runner

When I was twenty-five, I saw a movie called *The Loneliness of the Long Distance Runner,* in which a young man running for a reform school was far ahead in a cross-country race and then suddenly stopped as an act of rebellion. That young runner had been struck by the feeling that he had to go his own way and not the way demanded by society.

That young runner was me.

I hadn't been doing time, of course, just *marking* time at Temple, where my mind was not on books but bookings; and so, I had dropped out to go into show business, a career move as sound as seeking my future as a designer of dirigibles. Although my mother and father kept telling me that I should finish college before I flopped in show business, I felt that only *I*, with the full wisdom of a north Philadelphia jock, knew what was best for me. I empathized with the hero of *The Loneliness of the Long Distance Runner*, who had said about his race, "You have to run, run, run without knowing *why.*"

At twenty-five, I was certain that I knew where and why I wanted to run, so I switched to the track that led not to teaching children but to squelching drunks. I believed it was my destiny to make people laugh. These people, of course, did not include my mother and father, who felt that if there had been any value in stand-up comedy, Temple would have offered it for three credits. However, they could not change my mind: in spite of my previous plan to become a teacher, I now knew what a mistake teaching would have been for me and what a disservice I would have been doing to my students. At the start of each class, I would have been looking to see if the waiters were off the floor.

Thirteen years later, I had proved I was right. I was now thirty-eight, the father of four young children, and a man earning good money in show business. My home was in Massachusetts, but I was on the road for long periods, doing not just comedy in clubs but television and commercials too. And now, for the second time, I saw *The Loneliness of the Long Distance Runner,* and I found that its hero had not changed one bit in thirteen years: again he stopped running when he was clearly going to win the race. However, *I* had changed, and *this* time I thought:

Gee, that doesn't seem right. I wonder why he stopped. Did he have a bet on somebody else?

Perhaps he was bothered by the thought of being used to bring glory to a school and a system in which he didn't believe. Perhaps he was wondering what it felt like for a man *not* to win. Perhaps he had simply been overwhelmed by an urge to say, "The hell with it all."

At any rate, at this time of my life, when I was thirty-eight, my feeling toward this long distance dropout was a blend of sympathy and irritation. No longer did I see him as a heroic rebel: now I thought that he was merely misguided. He had been so far out in front that it would not have hurt for him to go on and win. Vince Lombardi may have been wrong when he said that winning was the *only* thing; however, it did still seem to me to be the point of a race. Getting there is *not* half the fun.

The third time I saw the film, I was forty-nine years old; and this time I saw its hero not as a courageous rebel or a misguided questioner of values, but simply as an old-fashioned son of a bitch. I felt this way because I was no longer the runner: I was now a man with a bet on the race—*five* bets, in fact—my children.

At forty-nine, I was trying to tell all these people that they should finish their formal education and then go on to be what they wanted to be. I was beginning to fear, however, that they would never *know* what they wanted to be, even when they got to *be* it. I am sorry if this thought is confusing; but while my children are trying to find themselves, I am allowed to be a little lost too.

And so, it was with the mind of this man, a man of forty-nine with five potential dropouts, that I saw *The Loneliness of the Long Distance Runner* for the third time. And *this* time, when that boy stopped running, I saw all five of my children giving up and I started to yell at the screen, choosing my words as carefully as a Doctor of Education should:

"You little *bastard!* You've had all the advantages of a good reform school and you're giving up like *that!* Well, I tell you this: I won't let *my* kids give up like that! They're all going to finish *college* before they become bums!"

And Thou, Beside Me for a Nap

I will not see this film again. I am fifty now and I'm tired. My hair is falling out and the highlight of my day is a nap and the water flows from a small ravine in my stomach after a shower. On the other hand, in spite of this flow, I can't moisturize the skin on my face as fast as it dries out. What I need is a canal from my stomach to my head.

What I also need is more time with my wife, to whom I want to be married until we forget each other's names. My wife is the only one who knows what I used to be; and she is starting to lose a little of it too, so we are breaking down in tandem.

"Either this room just got hotter or I picked up malaria in Central Park," she said to me one day last week.

"Don't be alarmed," I sweetly replied. "You're just going into training for menopause, but I'll be with you all the way. I won't blow hot and cold just because you happen to."

Dear, you have my promise: I will always be right there beside you, watching you clean out my medicine chest for the ninetieth time and then canceling another one of my orders for jalapeño pepper. And when I do have to go away to run on the treadmill at the Mayo Clinic, I'll be running to *you;* and I'll find you in a room with your friends: one of you fanning yourself, another one asking for a blanket, and a third one looking for locusts.

"Hello, ladies," I will say. "Hot and cold enough for you?"

Yes, I will even discuss the weather, in spite of the feeling I've always had that discussing the weather is a sign of growing old. But when my stomach ejects water like a sump pump while refusing to lubricate a pepper, the signs of growing old are flashing in neon, so it no longer matters what I say.

And when you have finished training for your menopause, I will take your hand and together we will walk back to my medicine chest one more time to see if you have missed anything I've saved from 1957. Of course, my *body* has saved nothing from 1957 except a few bones; but with you beside me, I am not interested in twenty anymore.

Twenty. A number to make a man sigh, to make a man dizzy with yearning.

"I can't change a twenty," a clerk says to me and I think, *Who can? They know it all and they have it all. The world is theirs.*

But, dear, I would never dream of leaving you for a woman of that age, a woman who didn't care if I saved leeches in my medicine chest or ate them with my peppers, a woman who thought that Miles Davis was a center for the Knicks and Lady Day was a holiday for women, a woman who wanted me to wear baggy pants and purple socks and a haircut that looked like a putting green, a woman who wanted me to party *past* the ten o'clock news. Dear, nobody knows better than you that I have reached the point in life where I can celebrate the arrival of the new year only when it arrives in another time zone, for a man of fifty is *in* another time zone, one where Henry Aaron and Charlie Parker still play.

The Today Show

When I began this book, my attitude toward aging was a blend of fighting and accepting it; but in the time it has taken me to write the book, I have gotten older and I'm doing a little more fighting than accepting right now.

"Dee-fense!" I am crying to joints that need 3-in-One Oil, to intestines that are begging for custard, and to eyes that are proud of their ability to distinguish day from night. However, I am also counting my blessings and not my time with a pointless pining for yesterday because I keep telling myself, "The older I get, the luckier I am."

Am I aging gracefully? Aging gracefully is for Baryshnikov; Cosby stumbles along, doing as well as he can and doing it in the here and now. The past is a ghost, the future a dream, and all we ever *have* is now. This philosophical flash may belong in a fortune cookie, but it's the best I can do at fifty. I do not know if the days are dwindling to a precious few for me or if I will make it to ninety-eight like my grandfather. Nonetheless, at fifty I am convinced that we must live as if we're immortal. The eminent scientist Linus Pauling says that in a way we *are* immortal because the body keeps renewing itself. And I am cheerfully with you, Linus—my legs are surely ripe for renewing—but you will pardon me if, once in a while, I behave like the *other* Linus and reach for my security blanket.